# Excel 2019 Formulas & Functions

### EXCEL ESSENTIALS 2019 BOOK 3

## M.L. HUMPHREY

Copyright © 2021 M.L. Humphrey

All Rights Reserved.

ISBN: 978-1-63744-032-2

# SELECT TITLES BY M.L. HUMPHREY

## EXCEL ESSENTIALS 2019

Excel 2019 Beginner

Excel 2019 Intermediate

Excel 2019 Formulas & Functions

Excel 2019 Formulas and Functions Study Guide

## WORD ESSENTIALS 2019

Word 2019 Beginner

Word 2019 Intermediate

## POWERPOINT ESSENTIALS 2019

PowerPoint 2019 Beginner

PowerPoint 2019 Intermediate

## ACCESS ESSENTIALS 2019

Access 2019 Beginner

Access 2019 Intermediate

# CONTENTS

| | |
|---|---:|
| **Introduction** | 1 |
| **How Formulas and Functions Work** | 3 |
| **Basic Math Calculations** | 7 |
| **Where To Find Functions** | 11 |
| **Best Practices** | 17 |
| **Copying Formulas** | 21 |
| **Top 10 Functions** | 25 |
|     The SUM Function | 26 |
|     The ROUND Function | 29 |
|     The RANDBETWEEN Function | 32 |
|     The CONVERT Function | 34 |
|     The TEXTJOIN Function | 37 |
|     The TRIM Function | 41 |
|     The TODAY Function | 43 |
|     The IFS Function | 45 |

# CONTENTS (CONT.)

| | |
|---|---|
| THE AND FUNCTION | 51 |
| THE VLOOKUP FUNCTION | 53 |

## BASE FUNCTIONS — 57

| | |
|---|---|
| THE AVERAGE FUNCTION | 58 |
| THE AVERAGEA FUNCTION | 60 |
| THE COUNT FUNCTION | 62 |
| THE MIN FUNCTION | 64 |
| THE MAX FUNCTION | 66 |

## LOGICAL* FUNCTIONS — 67

| | |
|---|---|
| THE OR FUNCTION | 68 |
| THE TRUE FUNCTION | 70 |
| THE NA FUNCTION | 71 |
| THE NOT FUNCTION | 72 |

## IF FUNCTIONS — 75

| | |
|---|---|
| THE IF FUNCTION | 77 |
| THE COUNTIFS FUNCTION | 80 |
| THE SUMIFS FUNCTION | 84 |
| THE AVERAGEIFS FUNCTION | 87 |
| THE MINIFS FUNCTION | 90 |

# CONTENTS (CONT.)

| | |
|---|---|
| THE MAXIFS FUNCTION | 92 |
| THE IFNA FUNCTION | 94 |
| THE IFERROR FUNCTION | 97 |
| **LOOKUP FUNCTIONS** | **99** |
| THE HLOOKUP FUNCTION | 100 |
| THE SWITCH FUNCTION | 103 |
| THE CHOOSE FUNCTION | 106 |
| THE TRANSPOSE FUNCTION | 108 |
| THE INDEX FUNCTION | 110 |
| THE MATCH FUNCTION | 116 |
| **STATISTICAL FUNCTIONS** | **119** |
| THE MEDIAN FUNCTION | 120 |
| THE MODE.SNGL FUNCTION | 122 |
| THE MODE.MULT FUNCTION | 123 |
| THE RANK.EQ FUNCTION | 126 |
| THE SMALL FUNCTION | 128 |
| THE FORECAST.LINEAR FUNCTION | 130 |
| THE FREQUENCY FUNCTION | 133 |
| **MORE MATH FUNCTIONS** | **137** |

# CONTENTS (CONT.)

    THE SUMPRODUCT FUNCTION — 138

    THE ABS FUNCTION — 140

    THE POWER FUNCTION — 141

    THE PI FUNCTION — 143

    THE LOG FUNCTION — 144

    THE FACT FUNCTION — 146

    THE COMBIN FUNCTION — 147

## TEXT FUNCTIONS — 149

    THE UPPER FUNCTION — 150

    THE LEFT FUNCTION — 151

    THE MID FUNCTION — 153

    THE TEXT FUNCTION — 154

    THE LEN FUNCTION — 156

    THE EXACT FUNCTION — 158

## DATE & TIME FUNCTIONS — 161

    THE DATE FUNCTION — 163

    THE YEAR FUNCTION — 167

    THE WEEKDAY FUNCTION — 169

    THE WEEKNUM FUNCTION — 171

## CONTENTS (CONT.)

| | |
|---|---:|
| THE EDATE FUNCTION | 173 |
| THE NETWORKDAYS.INTL FUNCTION | 174 |
| **OTHER FUNCTIONS** | **177** |
| **WHEN THINGS GO WRONG** | **179** |
| **CONCLUSION** | **183** |
| **APPENDIX A: CELL NOTATION** | **185** |
| **INDEX OF FUNCTIONS** | **187** |
| **ABOUT THE AUTHOR** | **189** |

# Introduction

Mastering formulas and functions in Excel will help you take what you can do with Excel to an entirely new level because many of the functions available in Excel (and we'll define what that means in the next chapter) allow you to shortcut tasks that would otherwise be very tedious or time-consuming.

For example, say you want to take units sold in Column A and price per unit in Column B and you want to determine the total earned across a hundred rows of data. If you did that manually, you'd have to type in =A1*B1 in Column C, copy that down all hundred rows, and then find a way to add all those values together, which, without the SUM function would require writing a formula that said =C1+C2+C3 all the way to +C100.

That's pretty time-consuming.

But there's a function that would do that for you called SUMPRODUCT. With SUMPRODUCT you can just write =SUMPRODUCT(A1:A100,B1:B100) and you're done.

So functions are valuable to learn because they save you a lot of time. And not just with numbers. I love the TRIM function which lets me remove excess spaces from around text entries, an issue that I've encountered more than once over the years, especially when breaking apart grouped data.

Now, are *you* going to need SUMPRODUCT? Maybe not. Maybe you never need TRIM either. Maybe you need some other functions within Excel that I barely ever use. There are certainly a wide variety of them.

That's why I saved formulas and functions for the last book in this series. Because formulas and functions are incredibly useful, but until you have some grounding in Excel you're not going to leverage them the way you could. You won't know what you can and can't do otherwise and how they fit into the bigger picture.

# M.L. Humphrey

In this book I cover approximately sixty functions in detail and touch upon about a hundred of them.

I've chosen functions most likely to be useful to a wide range of users but even then most users will probably only use two dozen functions on a regular basis, if that. So I can guarantee you right now that this book will cover at least one function you will never use and probably don't care about.

(The problem is, I don't know going in which ones you in particular need so we're going to cover some you don't in order to cover enough that you feel comfortable with all functions by the time we're done.)

Another thing to know before we start is that I am not doing this alphabetically.

I am going to start with ten of the most useful and/or representative functions (in my opinion), then cover the base functions and logical functions you need to effectively work with the various IF functions, and after that cover the actual IF functions. Then we'll move on to a sampling of functions under various categories such as Lookup Functions, Statistical Functions, Math Functions, Text Functions, and Date & Time Functions.

There is an index in the back that lists all of the functions mentioned in this book in alphabetical order if you're looking for one function in particular. The main sixty or so functions are listed in the table of contents up front.

(If you're reading in ebook you should be able to use the search function.)

While not every function will be useful to every reader of this book, at least be sure to read the introductory chapters and the chapters at the end that are generic to all formulas and functions and I do encourage you to read through up to the point where I mention that you can start skipping around.

As with the other books in this series, this book is written specifically for Excel 2019. If you're using an earlier version of Excel, *50 Useful Excel Functions* and *50 More Excel Functions,* which are part of the Excel Essentials series, my original series on Excel, were written to be more generic and are more comprehensive when read together. Functions that get a passing mention here get their own chapter in those books.

For the most part it won't matter which book you read, but this book does cover a few newer functions like IFS and TEXTJOIN that were not covered in those prior books.

Okay then, let's get started.

# How Formulas and Functions Work

For purposes of this book, we're going to define a formula in Excel as anything that is started with an equals sign and asks Excel to perform a calculation or task.

(Technically, as discussed in *Excel 2019 Beginner* you can start a formula with a plus or a minus sign as well, but I'm just going to ignore that because unless you're coming from a specific background where you learned to do things that way, you shouldn't do that. Also, Excel transforms those formulas into ones that use an equals sign anyway.)

I'm going to define a function as a command that is used within a formula to give instructions to Excel to perform a pre-defined task or set of tasks.

A function is basically agreed-upon shorthand.

So a formula in Excel could be as basic as:

$$=A1$$

It starts with an equals sign and is telling Excel that this particular cell where we've written our formula should have the exact same value as Cell A1. The "task" Excel completes here is pulling in that value.

But usually a formula will be more complex than that.

Look at the example I gave you above with SUMPRODUCT. (A function so I write it in capitals. All functions in this book will be written with capital letters.)

$$=SUMPRODUCT(A1:A100,B1:B100)$$

Still a formula, because we started with the equals sign and are asking Excel to perform a task. But in this case we've used the function SUMPRODUCT as shorthand to tell Excel that for every row in that range it should take the value from Column A and multiply it by the value in Column B and then should sum the resulting values and return the total.

Formulas can actually combine a large number of functions and calculations. For example the following formula combines two functions, TRIM and CONCAT, as well as four cell references, and four fixed values that indicate spaces:

=TRIM(CONCAT(A2," ",B2," ",C2," ",D2))

This is still a fairly simple formula. It can get much more complex. But as long as you can build the formula in the right way, Excel will perform all of the tasks you assign it.

The basic rules of building a formula are start with an equals sign and if you needed to use an opening paren make sure that it's paired with a closing paren.

All *functions* require the use of parens. You write the function name, the next thing you include is that opening paren, then you tell Excel the information it needs to perform that function (which varies by function), and then you end with a closing paren.

As you can see above with CONCAT, a function does not have to start a formula. It can and often will, but that is not a requirement.

For example, this is a perfectly legitimate formula that uses a function but starts with a cell reference instead:

=A1+SUM(B1:B5)

After you enter your formula in your cell, hit enter. (Or leave the cell by arrowing, using the tab key, or clicking away.)

The cell will then display the result of the formula. The formula will remain visible via the formula bar.

To see the formula that was used in a cell (if any), you can click on the cell and look to the formula bar.

Like so where I've clicked on Cell C1 which contains the formula =A1+B1:

# How Formulas and Functions Work

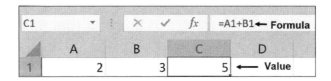

You can also double-click into the cell itself (Cell C1 here) and the cell will display the formula and also highlight any cells used in the formula. Like so:

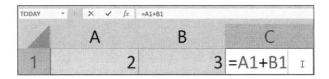

It's a little hard to see in print, but Cells A1 and B1 are highlighted in colors that match the color shown for their cell references in the formula in Cell C1. This makes it easy to see which cell is being used in which part of a formula, which becomes especially helpful when dealing with very complex formulas.

If you double-click on a cell to see the formula in the cell, exit the cell using Esc, Enter, tab or by clicking away. Do not arrow away because Excel may try to select a new range of cells to use in the formula instead of leaving the cell.

When you exit a cell with a formula, the cell will return to showing the calculated value.

With either method, the formula bar will always contain the formula for the cell you have selected.

Okay. Next we're going to take a quick detour into basic math calculations that don't require any functions at all, but are just simple formulas.

# Basic Math Calculations

Alright. Now let's take a quick detour with formulas before we go further with functions and walk through some basic math calculations that you can do without using a single function.

If I want to add two numerical values together in Excel, I could just go to any cell and type the formula into a cell using the plus sign (+) to indicate addition.

So here I'm adding 2 to 3:

$$=2+3$$

If those values were already showing in other cells, let's say Cells A1 and B1, I could write the formula to reference those cells instead:

$$=A1+B1$$

(If you aren't familiar with cell notation in Excel, see Appendix A.)

If I use cell notation, like in the second example there, then any change I make to the values in Cells A1 or B1 will also change the result of my formula because my formula is no longer performing a fixed calculation, like 2+3, but is instead performing a conditional calculation based on what's in Cells A1 and B1.

To subtract one number from another you use the minus (-) sign. To multiply two numbers you use the asterisk (*) sign. To divide two numbers you use the forward slash (/). So:

$$=3-2 \text{ would subtract 2 from 3}$$

=3*2 would multiply 3 times 2

=3/2 would divide 3 by 2

As I mentioned above, your formulas can either use cell references or numbers. So:

=A1-B1 would subtract the value in Cell B1 from the value in Cell A1

=A1*B1 would multiply the value in Cell A1 by the value in Cell B1

=A1/B1 would divide the value in Cell A1 by the value in Cell B1

Those are the most common non-function operators in Excel, but you can also use others such as the caret (^) symbol to indicate taking a value to a power. So:

=2^2 would be 2 times 2

=4^.5 would take the square root of 4

=3^3 would be 3 times 3 times 3

=27^(1/3) would take the cube root of 27

In that last example, by putting 1/3 in parens I told Excel to make that calculation first before take the root of 27.

If you're going to combine calculation steps within one cell, you need to be careful that you properly place your parens so that calculations are performed in the correct order.

There is a help document on this titled "Calculation operators and precedence in Excel" which you can find through the Help tab by searching for "order of precedence".

That help document lists the order in which calculations are done by Excel and also lists a number of operators (such as > for greater than) that are useful to know when working with formulas and functions in Excel. We'll cover those later as they come up in relation to certain functions like the IF function, but they're basically the same as you ran into in math class except you write >= and <= in Excel because there is no combined symbol for greater than or equal to or for less than or equal to.

If you're building a really complex formula it's always a good idea to test it as you go to make sure that all of the components are working properly and that the end result is the expected result. So I will build each component separately before combining them all in one cell.

But do check to see if there's a function that already does what you want. Especially when dealing with common calculations, there just might be. For example, there is a function for calculating net present value.

Also, before we move on to functions, remember the saying "garbage in, garbage out". Excel is not a person. It can't read your mind and know what you meant, all it can do is take what you give it and return the result. So always, always gut check any result you get from Excel. Does that actually make sense?

I will often double-check a complex formula by creating the same calculation two different ways to see if the result is the same.

For example, with the net present value function, when first working with it, I'll also do that calculation old school in Excel using basic math like we just discussed to see if I get the same result both ways. Once I'm comfortable that I'm giving Excel the right inputs, then I can stop doing that.

Also, if you give Excel the wrong kind of inputs or fail to give Excel the inputs it needs, you will get an error message. We discuss the types of error messages at the end, but in the meantime if you do get an error message I'd suggest that you check that the data in your formula is formatted as the right data type, confirm that you have matching opening and closing parens, and verify (for a function) that you provided all of the required inputs. That's usually where things go wrong.

Alright. Next we'll talk about where to find functions in Excel.

# Where To Find Functions

In this book we're going to cover approximately one hundred Excel functions, sixty in detail, that I thought were most useful for the largest number of people. But there are far, far more functions than that in Excel, and chances are at some point you'll need one I didn't cover here.

To find the functions available in Excel, you can go to the Formulas tab. There is a section called Function Library that lists various categories of functions. Mine shows Recently Used, Financial, Logical, Text, Date & Time, Lookup & Reference, Math & Trig, and then there's a dropdown for More Functions that shows the categories Statistical, Engineering, Cube, Information, Compatibility, and Web.

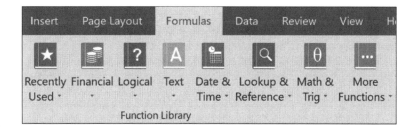

Click on the dropdown arrow next to any of the categories and you'll see a listing of functions that fall under that heading.

Now, unless you know what you're looking for, this listing probably won't help you much because the functions are named things like ACCRINT and IFNA.

You can hold your cursor over each of the names and Excel will provide a brief description of the function for you, but for some of the lists that's a lot of functions to look through.

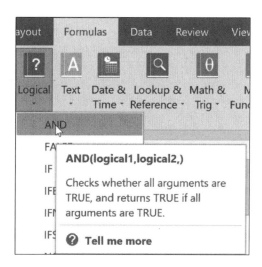

Each description also includes a Tell Me More at the end of the description. If you click on that option, the Excel Help task pane will appear. You can then click on the category for the function (in this case Logical) and then choose the function from the list you see there.

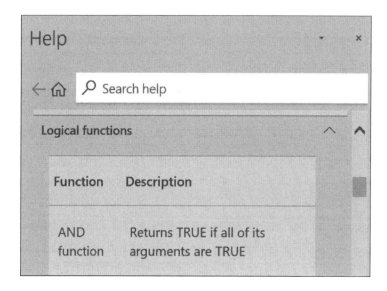

This will bring up an additional set of information specific to that function that will generally include the definition for that function as well as examples and further discussion of how the function works and any limitations it might have. The complexity of the help varies by function.

# Where To Find Functions

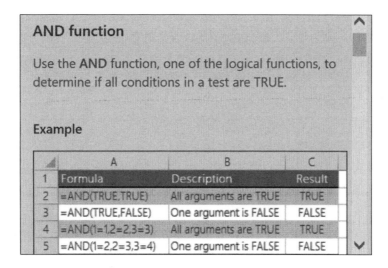

That will give you information on a function, but I do it differently because I'm usually looking to use a function.

Instead, what I do is click into my cell and then use the Insert Function option available on the far left hand side of the Formulas tab.

Clicking on Insert Function will bring up the Insert Function dialogue box.

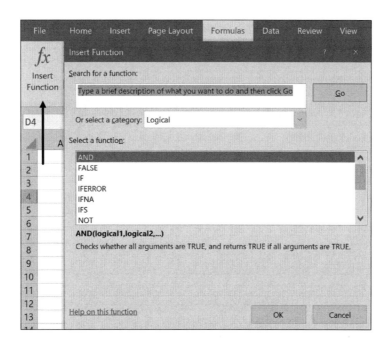

In the top section under where it says "Search for a function" you can type what you're looking to do and then click on Go. (Be sure that the category dropdown right below the search box is set to All unless you know for sure what category your function falls under.)

Excel will provide a list of functions that it thinks meet your search criteria. (Sometimes this list is very far off, so don't just accept the first choice blindly.) You can left-click on each of the listed functions to see a brief description of the function directly below the box where the functions are listed.

You will also see in the description for each function a list of the required inputs for that function as well.

For AND you can see in the screenshot above that it requires at least two logical inputs but allows for more and that it is described as a function that "Checks whether all arguments are TRUE, and returns TRUE if all arguments are TRUE."

For every function we cover in this book I will list that description that you see right there at the very top of the section.

If you need more information on a function, you can click on the "Help on this function" link in the bottom left corner of the dialogue box which will bring up a website specific to that function.

Otherwise, you can just click on the function you want and choose OK.

This will insert the function into whichever cell you'd been clicked into before you chose Insert Function. You will also see a Function Arguments dialogue box that lists the inputs your function needs and provides a location for you to input those values so that Excel can build your formula for you.

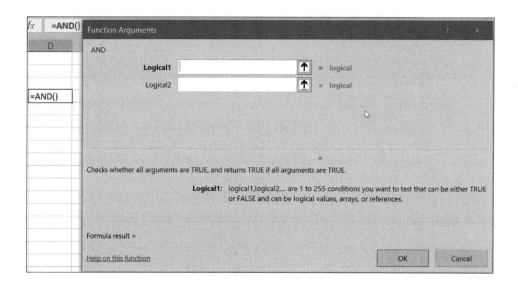

# Where To Find Functions

You can use the dialogue box if it helps or close it out by clicking on OK and then OK on the error dialogue box and then typing in the values directly into the formula bar or cell that you want to use which will now contain the function minus its required inputs. So =AND() as an example.

If you use the dialogue box, you can either input numeric values in those boxes or use cell references by clicking on the cells in your worksheet or typing the cell references in.

At the bottom of the list of inputs Excel will show you a sample value based upon the inputs you've chosen. The sample also appears in the bottom left corner of the dialogue box.

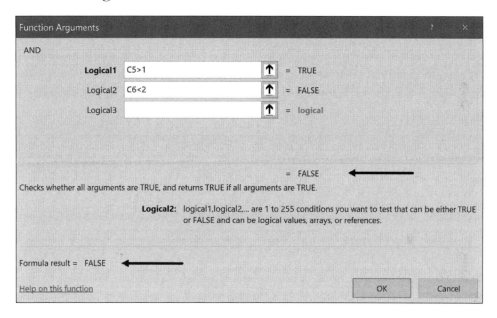

Even with the help of the Function Arguments dialogue box, sometimes you still need to know what a function is doing in order to get a result that makes any sort of sense. In this case, to get the AND function to really work I had to put more than just cell references into the input boxes. I had to give it criteria to apply to those values.

(We'll talk about this more when we discuss the AND function, but what's happening up there is that I'm asking Excel to tell me if both the value in Cell C5 is greater than 1 and the value in Cell C6 is less than 2. Because both of those are not true, the answer it's giving is FALSE. )

If you use the dialogue box, when you're done, click OK and the calculated value will appear in your cell.

You can always go back to the cell and edit the formula either through the formula bar or by double-clicking on the cell.

\* \* \*

If you already know the function you want to use but aren't sure about the required inputs, you can start typing the function into your formula in a cell in your worksheet. As you type the function name Excel will suggest functions in a list below the cell and for the selected function name will show a definition for that function like it's doing below for the AND function.

After you type the opening paren for the function you want, Excel will then show the required inputs for that function and their required order.

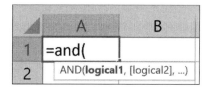

If you click on the function name in that small pop-up box after you've typed the opening paren, Excel will open the Excel Help task pane specific to that function.

\* \* \*

If none of that works to help you find the function you need, then an Internet search is probably your best option.

A quick search for something like "How do I get Excel to identify the day of the week from a date?" will usually get you the answer you need. You can then use one of the above options to learn more.

# Best Practices

Now let's discuss a few best practices when it comes to using formulas and functions.

## Make Your Assumptions Visible

You can easily build a formula where all of the information to make the calculation is contained within that one cell.

So if I want to add the values 10, 20, and 30 together I can do that in one cell using =10+20+30 and all anyone will see in the worksheet is the result of that calculation, 60.

You may be tempted to do this because it's clean. All that people see is what you want them to, the result of your calculation.

And maybe you don't expect to have to adjust those values so you don't see an issue in having your formula built that way.

I would encourage you not to do this. In my experience, a best practice in terms of building formulas is to have any fixed values or assumptions visible in the worksheet. The reason to do this is so that someone looking at the sheet can see what assumptions fed the calculation.

Here's an example:

Let's say you're calculating how much you'll make if you sell your house. You figure you'll have to spend $2,500 to clean the place up a bit, pay a commission of 5%, and that the house is worth $500,000.

Now, if you sat down to discuss this with your spouse you could just show them the results of that calculation (the value on the left below) or you could show them the results of the calculation and the assumptions you made (the value on the right).

|   | B | C | D | E |
|---|---|---|---|---|
| 1 | Option 1 | | | Option 2 |
| 2 | | | Home Price | $500,000.00 |
| 3 | $472,500.00 | | Commission | 5% |
| 4 | | | Fix Up Cost | $2,500.00 |
| 5 | | | | |
| 6 | | | Net | $472,500.00 |

Depending on your spouse, they still might want to see the formula, but at least here they can see the assumed sales price, commission, and fix-up cost and say, "That doesn't seem right. Houses in the area like ours have been selling for $400,000 not $500,000 and the neighbors up the street worked with a great broker who only charges 4% commission."

Without showing them your assumptions, they aren't given a chance to provide their input.

Also, even if it's just for you, if you bury your assumptions in your calculation field they're easy to forget about. That can be dangerous if they're wrong or circumstances change.

## Use Paste Special - Values

The other thing I do that you may or may not want to do depending on why you're using Excel is that I frequently use Paste Special – Values when I'm done with performing a set of calculations.

Do not do this if the calculations you performed need to be updated on an ongoing basis.

But I do a lot of calculations where I want to keep the results for reference but will not be recalculating any values, and I want to lock those values down so that I don't lose them or inadvertently recalculate them by changing a value in an input cell or deleting data that fed those calculations.

(Deleting data I used in a calculation to tidy things up and turning my calculation fields into error messages is something I do far too often.)

The simple way to do this is to select the cells, use Ctrl + C to copy, and then right-click and under Paste Special choose the Values option (the one with the 123 on the clipboard). This will replace any calculated cells in that range with just the values of the calculation.

You basically just copy your formulas and paste the results from the formulas right on top.

After you do that, instead of a formula, for example, =A1+B1, you'll have a cell that just contains the result of having added Cells A1 and B1 together. That means if you then delete the values in Cells A1 and B1 it won't change the cell with the result in it.

## Don't Mess With Your Raw Data

I mentioned this in the other books, but am going to mention it again here because it is so, so important.

To the extent possible, you should always store your raw data in one location and do all of your calculations and manipulations on that data elsewhere.

(Ideally you would also record all of the steps you followed to take that raw data and turn it into your final product, but it's not as easy to do in something like Excel as it is in a program like R where you are basically writing a script of steps to follow.)

If you don't keep your raw data untouched all it takes is one bad sort or one bad function and your data can be irreparably changed in a way you can't fix after the fact. Usually you can undo if you notice it immediately, but chances are you won't.

If, on the other hand, you keep your raw data separate, there is nothing you can't come back from. You might have to redo a lot of work, but you won't be left with a data set that's useless.

I also save versions of my worksheets when I'm working on something particularly complicated. That way I can go back to a stage where everything was working without having to start over from scratch. Just be sure to label your files clearly so that you know which is the most recent version. (File V1, File V2, etc.)

## Test Your Formulas

I think I already touched on this one earlier, but let's cover it again.

If I'm going to apply a formula to a large range of data I will usually test that formula on a much smaller sample of my data where I can visually evaluate the results.

So if I'm writing a formula to sum customer transactions for customers from Alaska who bought Widgets (using SUMIFS), I'll run that formula against just ten rows of data to make sure that it's doing what I think it should before I apply it to ten thousand rows of data.

As much as possible you should always either check you formulas on a subset of data or "gut check" your results. Don't just accept the value Excel gives you without questioning whether it actually makes sense. (Because garbage in, garbage out. Excel's ability to perform calculations is limited by your ability to write those calculations properly, and we all make mistakes. One missing $ sign or one > instead of >= and the result you get will not be the result you wanted.)

Be especially wary when it comes to edge cases. Those are the situations where you want the results that are equal to or greater than 25, say. In that situation the edge case would be when the value is 25, 24.99, or 25.01. You want to check that those all give the result you expected.

(I personally have a bad habit of wanting 25 or greater and writing the formula as greater than 25 and having to go back and fix it when I realize my mistake)

So, test, test, test. And then check, check, check.

## Consider Your Audience

I've said this before and I'll say it again and I will keep saying it forever. When creating anything in Excel, keep your audience in mind. I once created a beautiful workbook that did lots of complex calculations for a consulting client. It was a masterpiece. Only problem was, they didn't have the version of Excel I did and I'd used a function (SUMIFS) that didn't exist in their version of Excel. So that thing of beauty I created? Worthless. I had to go back and re-create the same calculations without using SUMIFS. It was a painful but valuable lesson.

Less likely to happen these days with Microsoft 365, but still something that could happen. So if you're going to share Excel files with people outside your organization be very careful what functions you use to create whatever you're going to share. Make sure they're backwards compatible as much as you possibly can. I think we're about at the end of needing to save files as .xls files, but there's still the issue of number of rows in each version of Excel, functions used, filtering used, etc. that can really trip you up if you're not careful.

# Copying Formulas

Before we move into discussing specific functions, I want to cover how to copy formulas and how to keep cell references fixed. I covered this before in *Excel 2019 Beginner*, but it's well worth discussing again because the way in which formulas copy in Excel is key to what makes them so powerful.

That's because you can write a formula once, copy it, and paste it to thousands of cells, and Excel will automatically adjust that formula to its new location

It's fantastic.

But the default for copying formulas is that every single cell reference in the formula adjusts for the new location of the formula.

So if the original formula was in the first cell of the third column (otherwise known as Cell C1) and was written to add the value in the first cell of the first column to the value in the first cell of the second column (otherwise known as =A1+B1) then when you copy that formula over to the second row of the sixth column (Cell F2) everything in the formula will adjust by three columns and one row as well (so that you now have =D2+E2).

Great when that's exactly what you want. Horrible if you're working with any fixed values.

There's something I often like to build for my own analysis that's called a two-variable analysis grid that takes two inputs and calculates the potential combinations of the two.

For example, given a variety of hours worked per week and money earned per hour worked, what are the possible amounts you could earn?

Or, given various sales prices for a home and various commission rates, what could you earn from selling your home? What about if you included a fix-up cost in that calculation?

To do these calculations properly requires telling Excel to keep certain portions of the cell reference in your formula fixed.

You do this by using a $ sign.

So let's just build this right now so you can see it at work using the mortgage example above. That will let us demonstrate all three ways to use the $ sign to fix or partially fix cell references.

Here's our set-up. We haven't done the calculations yet, but I've put in the numbers we're going to use. We want to see what the different outcomes are if the house sells for between $400,000 and $500,000 and when we have to pay a sales commission of 3% to 6%. This only works with two variables the way I have it set up so we're assuming that fix-up costs are set at $2,500.

|   | A | B | C | D | E | F | G |
|---|---|---|---|---|---|---|---|
| 1 | Fix-Up Cost | $2,500.00 | | | | | |
| 2 | | | | | House Sale Price | | |
| 3 | | | $400,000 | $425,000 | $450,000 | $475,000 | $500,000 |
| 4 | Commission to Realtor | 3% | | | | | |
| 5 | | 4% | | | | | |
| 6 | | 5% | | | | | |
| 7 | | 6% | | | | | |

First, we write the formula for Cell C4 using the values in Cells B1, C3, and B4.

$$=(C3*(1-B4))-B1$$

That's saying take our sale price on the home (C3) and reduce it by the commission amount (B4).

(The way to reduce it by the commission amount is to use 100% minus the commission, in this case 3%, to get our net amount to us of 97%.)

And then with the money we earn from the sale, pay for our fix-up costs (B1).

You could re-write that formula for each and every cell, but who wants to?

Instead, we're going to copy the formula to all the other cells. But first we have to tell Excel to keep certain parts of the formula fixed.

For fix-up costs, B1, we want that to not change at all. It will always be the value in Cell B1. We write that using $ signs in front of both the column and row portion of the cell reference, so $B$1 means never change the B or the 1 as the formula is copied.

# Copying Formulas

The house sale price is trickier. Because when we copy our formula to Columns D, E, F, and G we do want the column reference to change, but not the row reference. To accomplish that we replace the C3 with C$3. That keeps taking the values from Row 3 but lets the column change.

With the commission value as we copy to rows 5, 6, and 7 we want the columns to stay fixed, but the row numbers to change. To accomplish that we replace the B4 with $B4. That keeps the value in Column B but lets the row change.

Our new formula becomes:

$$=(C\$3*(1-\$B4))-\$B\$1$$

And when we copy it to the rest of the cells in that table, all of the calculations work correctly for that combination of values.

| | A | B | C | D | E | F | G |
|---|---|---|---|---|---|---|---|
| 1 | Fix-Up Cost | $2,500.00 | | | | | |
| 2 | | | | | House Sale Price | | |
| 3 | | | $400,000 | $425,000 | $450,000 | $475,000 | $500,000 |
| 4 | Commission to Realtor | | 3% | $385,500 | $409,750 | $434,000 | $458,250 | $482,500 |
| 5 | | | 4% | $381,500 | $405,500 | $429,500 | $453,500 | $477,500 |
| 6 | | | 5% | $377,500 | $401,250 | $425,000 | $448,750 | $472,500 |
| 7 | | | 6% | $373,500 | $397,000 | $420,500 | $444,000 | $467,500 |

I can double-click into Cell G7 and see that the formula in that cell is:

$$=(G\$3*(1-\$B7))-\$B\$1$$

And that the correct cells are being referenced for that particular calculation. We're still referencing Cell B1 but now we reference Cells G3 and B7.

A two-variable analysis grid is incredibly useful and will come in handy in any number of analysis scenarios. (Units sales and price is another one that comes to mind.) And to build one with ease relies completely on this particular trick.

Another time when I find that I need to be careful about cell references when I'm copying a formula is when I'm dealing with cell ranges.

Sometimes I'll want to look at a value as a percent of the total and I'll use a formula that references the specific range of values instead of the entire column, maybe because I have a grand total row at the bottom that would interfere with just using the entire column. So I'll use an equation like:

$$=A1/SUM(A1:A25)$$

The problem comes when I copy that to Cell A2 and and not only does my A1 in the beginning of the formula adjust to become A2, which I want, but my A1:A25 in the second part of the formula becomes A2:A26, which I don't.

So a scenario like that requires writing the formula like so:

$$=A1/SUM(\$A\$1:\$A\$25)$$

That lets the A1 in the first part of the formula change, but keeps the referenced cell range in the second part of the formula fixed.

(In this specific scenario I can check that my calculation is working by taking the total of all of my calculations which should add up to 1 or 100%.)

Also, if you just need to move a formula to a new location but don't want any of the cell references to adjust then remember to cut and move the formula instead of copying it.

You can either click on the cell and use Ctrl + X if you don't need to leave the formula in its original location.

Or, if you do want to keep the formula in its original location as well but don't want it to change, click on the cell, go to the formula bar, highlight the formula there, copy it, hit Esc, go to the new cell, and then paste using Ctrl + V or Paste in the Home tab. (Enter doesn't work for this one.)

OK. That's it for the preliminaries. Time to start talking about specific functions. We'll start with ten of the most useful functions first, which I've chosen to give you a good idea of what's possible in Excel as well as based upon how often I've used them or will use them going forward (since a couple were only introduced recently.)

# Top 10 Functions

Alright, we're going to start with ten key functions that I've chosen either because I use them all the time and think others will as well (SUM is probably the most commonly-used function if I had to guess), or because I think they're useful and representative of the power and variety of functions within Excel.

A few of these are either new or close to new but if you're only going to be working in Excel 2019 and don't need backwards compatibility they are incredibly powerful and worth learning. For example, I would have in the past put IF on this list but in Excel 2019 I'm putting IFS which is a newer function that has the potential to largely take the place of the IF function.

Same with TEXTJOIN. In the past I would have used CONCAT (which used to be CONCATENATE) to do what TEXTJOIN now does and does with far less effort involved.

Okay, let's get started with SUM.

# The SUM Function

**Notation:** SUM(number1, [number2],…)

**Excel Definition:** Adds all the numbers in a range of cells.

The SUM function is probably the most basic function in Excel and I'd suspect the most widely used. What the SUM function does is add numbers together. These can be numbers that you type directly into the function (not recommended as discussed above under best practices) or they can be values that are stored in other cells. Cells do not need to be touching for their values to be added together, although it's much easier to write your SUM function if they are.

To use the function you use SUM and must include at least one number (or cell range) within the parens.

Some examples of formulas that use the SUM function are:

$$=SUM(2,3,4)$$

This adds the numbers 2, 3, and 4 together. So it's the same as using =2+3+4 as your formula.

$$=SUM(A1,A2,A3)$$

This formula does the exact same thing as the first formula except it's using cell references to add the values in Cells A1, A2, and A3 together. You could also type =A1+A2+A3 in a cell and get the same result.

$$=SUM(A1:A3)$$

This is where the SUM function becomes necessary. It's a cleaner way to write the second example since we've replaced A1, A2, A3 with A1:A3 which is saying "Cells A1 *through* A3." Because of the cell notation it requires use of the SUM function to work. For three cells it's not that big of a difference, but what about:

=SUM(A1:A100)

Now you can see where the SUM function comes in very, very handy because with one small function we can sum all the values in Cells A1 through A100.

Here's an example that uses two different ranges of cells:

=SUM(A1:A3,B2:B6)

This one is saying to add all the values in the range from Cell A1 to Cell A3 (so Cells A1, A2, and A3) as well as all the values in the range from Cell B2 to Cell B6 (so Cells B2, B3, B4, B5, and B6). Because of the use of the cell ranges, this one also requires use of the SUM function. The alternative would be to write =A1+A2+A3+B2+B3+B4+B5+B6 which no one wants to do.

=SUM(A:A)

This example is saying to sum all of the values in Column A.

=SUM(5:5)

And this one is summing all of the values in Row 5.

\* \* \*

Neither of those last two can be easily replaced with a formula that uses the plus sign. They demonstrate just how powerful such a simple function can be.

So, pretty simple, right?

Start with an equals sign, SUM, opening paren, whatever you want to add together using cell notation, closing paren. Done.

And as I mentioned above, you can also combine functions in a larger formula. So, for example, if I had a value in Cell A1 and I wanted to subtract all of the values in Column C, I could write that as:

=A1-SUM(C:C)

Or if I wanted to subtract the values in Column C from A1 but then also add the values in Column E, I could do that as well:

$$=A1-SUM(C:C)+SUM(E:E)$$

Note that when a function doesn't start a formula that you don't need to put the equals sign in front of it.

Alright.

Next up is ROUND.

# The ROUND Function

**Notation:** ROUND(number, num_digits)

**Excel Definition:** Rounds a number to a specified number of digits.

ROUND is a simple but potentially useful function. It takes a value and rounds that value to a specified number of digits.

(You can use the formatting options in Excel to give the appearance of having rounded a number. So Number or Currency or Accounting will all format a number to show two decimal places, but using the ROUND function actually transforms the number so that it now only has that number of decimal places.)

The inputs into the ROUND function are the value you want to round and then the number of digits to round that number to.

If you use 0 for the number of digits the number will be rounded to the nearest integer. So

$$=\text{ROUND}(111.2345,0)$$

rounds the number 111.2345 zero digits and will return 111 as the value.

If you use a positive number, such as 2, for num_digits the number will be rounded to that many decimal places. So

$$=\text{ROUND}(111.2345,2)$$

rounds 111.2345 to two decimal places and will return 111.23 as the value.

If you use a negative number for num_digits, such as -2, the number will be rounded to that number of 10's, 100's, 1000's places, etc. So

$$=\text{ROUND}(111.2345,-2)$$

will round 111.2345 negative 2 digits and return a result of 100.

ROUND does not force a specific number of decimal places on a number, however.

For example, if I use

$$=\text{ROUND}(1.23,4)$$

which means to round the number 1.23 to the fourth decimal place, ROUND will return a value of 1.23 not 1.2300. (You would need to use TEXT to enforce that type of formatting or you would need to format your cells that way using one of the number formatting options.)

The way Excel decides whether to round up or round down is by looking at the digit one past the one you're going to keep. If that digit is a 0 through a 4, Excel will round down. (Thus keeping the rest of the number unchanged.) If that digit is a 5 through a 9, Excel will round up and the final digit that you're keeping will go up by one.

This is easier to understand if we look at some examples:

$$=\text{ROUND}(1.234,2)$$

says to change the number 1.234 to a number with just two decimal places. So the question is does that become 1.23 or 1.24? The answer is 1.23 because the digit one past the 3, which is the last digit we're keeping, is a 4. Since that value is in the lower range, 0 through 4, we round down.

$$=\text{ROUND}(1.235,2)$$

says the same thing and we have the same two choices, 1.23 or 1.24. But now our last digit after the one we're keeping is a 5 so we round up and our final value becomes 1.24.

Where it gets interesting, for me, is when you have multiple numbers that you're not keeping. So

$$=\text{ROUND}(1.2347,2)$$

says to convert 1.2347 to a number with two decimal places as well. If you started at the end and rounded each number at a time you would go from 1.2347 to 1.235 to 1.24. But that's not how Excel works. (And not how rounding in general works either. I looked it up.)

As I explained above, Excel takes the 1.23 that we want to keep and ONLY looks at the next digit in the number. In this case that's a 4 so Excel would round down and return a value of 1.23.

So there you have it. That's how ROUND works.

If you want to force the direction in which your value is rounded, you can use ROUNDUP or ROUNDDOWN. If you don't want to round at all but just want to cut the number off at a specific point, you can use the TRUNC function. The INT function will round a number down to the nearest whole number (integer).

Okay. Now let's move on to RANDBETWEEN.

# The RANDBETWEEN Function

**Notation:** RANDBETWEEN(bottom, top)

**Excel Definition:** Returns a random number between the numbers you specify.

Sometimes when working with data you need to have a random start. For example, if I want to sample a series of transactions and be able to extrapolate my results to that entire population of transactions, I need to start at a random point and then take every nth transaction from that point forward until I've worked my way through the entire sample back to my starting point.

You can use a function like RAND or RANDBETWEEN to choose that random value. The RAND function can be used to randomly generate a value between 0 and 1, but I chose to cover RANDBETWEEN here because it allows you to specify a range of values to use for your random number generation, and the number it returns is always a whole number which makes it the more useful function for taking samples or choosing from a numbered population.

So say I have a set of 532 transactions I need to sample and want to know which transaction to randomly start with. I can write:

=RANDBETWEEN(1,532)

When I hit enter, Excel will show me a random whole number between 1 and 532. I can then use this number to identify my starting transaction.

Be careful though. Because every time you press F9, make a new calculation in your worksheet, or reopen your worksheet it will calculate a new random value. And once it does that there's no way to go back to your prior value. Ctrl + Z will not work. That number is gone and it's not coming back.

So if you use RANDBETWEEN and you need to record the random number Excel generates, which you likely will, use copy and paste special – values to store the value as a number. Or you could build a process that acts on that value as soon as it's generated.

Another option to lock in your result is to click on the cell with your formula in it, highlight the RANDBETWEEN( ) portion of the formula, hit F9, and then hit Enter. That will lock in the calculation as of that moment in time. (This trick works with any portion of a formula as long as you can select the entire function name, the opening paren, the argument, and the closing paren.)

Be forewarned though that paste special-values and the F9 + Enter trick both leave you with a fixed value and get rid of the function entirely.

Now on to the CONVERT function.

# The CONVERT Function

**Notation:** CONVERT(number, from_unit, to_unit)

**Excel Definition:** Converts a number from one measurement system to another.

CONVERT is an incredibly useful function that will allow you to easily convert from one measurement to another.

(Let me note here that if the conversion you need is just a one-off you can easily use an internet browser to do this. Just type in "20 degree Celsius to Fahrenheit" in the search bar and hit enter, for example, and the top result or one of the top results will be the answer. But if you have a range of values you need to convert or you need to keep doing this conversion on a regular basis, then this function is the way to do it)

In the help text for the function there is a very long list of options for what you can convert spread across the following categories: weight and mass, distance, time, pressure, force, energy, power, magnetism, temperature, volume (or liquid measure), area, information (bits to bytes), and speed. In addition there is a list of prefixes and binary prefixes that can be prepended to any of the metrics to change the magnitude of the value.

The function itself is very easy to use. The hardest part of using it is knowing what abbreviation to use for your from_unit and to_unit options. You can find all of the available abbreviations in the Help text dialogue box for the function or you can just start entering your function and look at the options provided when you reach each input field.

For example, when you reach the from_unit option you'll see a dropdown menu of the available measurements and you can just scroll down and double-click on the one you need. Same with when you reach the to_unit portion of the function. If you do it this way, the to_unit portion will only display the available options that are in the same category as the from_unit option, saving you the potential of having an error due to type mismatch between your from units and to units.

Let's walk through a few straight-forward examples:

I have a number of friends who live overseas and are always talking about how hot it is there, because it's 40 degrees out. Now, being from Colorado you tell me that it's 40 degrees out I'm bundling up before I head outside. This is because my friends are talking about Celsius temperatures and I'm talking about Fahrenheit temperatures.

So to find what 40 degrees Celsius is in Fahrenheit temperature, you could use:

$$=CONVERT(40,"C","F")$$

(That's 104 degrees Fahrenheit and, yes, I'd agree that's pretty darned hot.)

It's as simple as that. The first part of the function is the value you need to convert, the next part is its current units, and the final part is the unit of measurement you need to convert to.

Note that the abbreviation for the measurement has to be in quotes and is case-sensitive.

What about if you know an event is occurring in 1,200 days but aren't sure how many years from now that will be?

You can just use:

$$=CONVERT(1200,"day","yr")$$

Result? 3.285

Those are just two very simple uses for CONVERT. I'll note here that it's listed as an Engineering function and you can see that it might be useful in a context like that if you scroll through the list of available conversion options as well as the list of prefixes that are available.

Make sure your units to and from are in the same category or you'll get a #N/A error. Same with if you try to use a measurement abbreviation that doesn't exist. This includes if you input the value using the wrong case. So "day" is a valid unit value, but "Day" is not.

Let me add here, too, that even though it's not on the list of available options you can use "km" for kilometers. Also, "mi" is the miles option you want if you're just trying to convert a good old standard mile to a different distance measurement. (The Help text refers to "mi" as a statute mile.)

Also, in the Help dialogue box they show how to handle squared units by doubling the CONVERT function. So to convert 100 square feet into square meters they say to use:

$$=\text{CONVERT}(\text{CONVERT}(100,"ft","m"),"ft","m")$$

By nesting the two CONVERT functions that way it appears to work to convert a squared unit to a squared unit.

(I tested it with squared inches to squared feet and it worked on that as well, I'm just using hedging language here because I haven't personally thought through *why* that works the way it does. I'm sure someone more mathematically inclined than I am could write up a little mathematical proof to show me why that works that way, but suffice it to say it does.)

# The TEXTJOIN Function

**Notation:** TEXTJOIN(delimiter, ignore_empty, text1, [text2],...)

**Excel Definition:** Concatenates a list or range of text strings using a delimiter.

This function is new in Excel 2019. Previously I would have used CONCATENATE or CONCAT to accomplish the same task, but with a lot more angst and effort.

What TEXTJOIN does is takes text entries in multiple cells or in a list that you provide and combines them into one cell. If you specify a delimiter it will use that delimiter between each of the values that you want combined. You can also tell Excel to ignore any cell that is empty or to include it anyway.

Beautiful.

So how would you use this? Why put it here?

One of the things I've had to do in the past is take entries such as first name, middle name, last name, suffix, and combine them to form one single entry. So instead of Mary, Jo, Jones I want to create an entry that reads Mary Jo Jones.

TEXTJOIN makes this very easy to do. In this scenario we want a space as our delimiter which we can represent using " " where the space is in the quotes. And because some people won't have middle names we want to tell Excel to ignore empty cells, which means we use a 1 for TRUE. (Or you can just use TRUE.)

So let's do this. Here's my sample data:

|   | A | B | C | D |
|---|---|---|---|---|
| 1 | First | Middle | Last | Suffix |
| 2 | Mary | Jo | Jones | |
| 3 | Mark | | Allen | Jr |
| 4 | Elizabeth | | Zhan | |

In Cell E2 I can add a TEXTJOIN function that reads:

$$=\text{TEXTJOIN}(" ",1,A2:D2)$$

And then copy that down for Rows 3 and 4. The A2:D2 is my range of values that I want Excel to combine. When I copy that down that will change for each row.

Here are the results:

| | A | B | C | D | E |
|---|---|---|---|---|---|
| 1 | **First** | **Middle** | **Last** | **Suffix** | **TEXTJOIN** |
| 2 | Mary | Jo | Jones | | Mary Jo Jones |
| 3 | Mark | | Allen | Jr | Mark Allen Jr |
| 4 | Elizabeth | | Zhan | | Elizabeth Zhan |

Easy enough.

There is a limit on the function but it's pretty high. You can't have more than 32,767 characters or else you'll get a #VALUE! error message.

The delimiter I gave it above was a blank space, but if you wanted to do a list of values separated by a comma you would use ", " instead which puts a comma as well as a space for the delimiter.

If you do use something like a comma and space for the delimiter and choose not to ignore blanks you can end up with something fairly unattractive where you have , , , if there are missing values.

The help text for this function shows an interesting way to provide a cell range instead of a single delimiter to handle a situation where you need multiple delimiters. In their example they use three commas and then a semi-colon as their delimiters by referencing a cell range that contains those marks.

It works in their sample because all of the data had the same number of inputs. There was a city, state, zip code, and country in every line of data and there were not blanks.

But applying it to our scenario above to try to add a comma before the suffix, I got weird results. This is because I have entries where the number of values in the end result are the same, but the third value is a suffix for one line (Mark Allen, Jr) and a last name for another (Mary Jo Jones). When you use a cell range to specify the delimiter what you're doing is telling Excel that the first delimiter is in the first cell of the range, the second delimiter is in the second cell of the range, etc.

So if I take the middle name value for Mary Jo Jones out of my data above, I can get this to work. Like so:

| | A | B | C | D | E |
|---|---|---|---|---|---|
| | | | | | =TEXTJOIN($A$12:$B$12,1,A7:D7) |
| 6 | First | Middle | Last | Suffix | TEXTJOIN |
| 7 | Mary | | Jones | | Mary Jones |
| 8 | Mark | | Allen | Jr | Mark Allen, Jr |
| 9 | Elizabeth | | Zhan | | Elizabeth Zhan |
| 10 | | | | | |
| 11 | First Delimiter | Second Delimiter | | | |
| 12 | | , | | | |

What I've done is in Cell A12 I've added a space. And in Cell B12 I've added a comma and a space. I've then changed the formula to:

$$=TEXTJOIN(\$A\$12:\$B\$12,1,A7:D7)$$

I use the $ signs so that I can copy that formula to the other rows and not lose the fixed reference to my delimiters that are in Cells A12 and B12. Only Cell E8 needs a second delimiter so it's the only one that uses the comma. This only works because I said TRUE (1) for ignoring empty cells. If I'd used FALSE (0) instead, I'd have

Mary , Jones

Mark , Allen Jr

Elizabeth , Zhan

Which brings up an interesting quirk in using a range of delimiters. And that's that if you have more delimiters needed than you provided in the list, Excel will go back to the beginning and start using the delimiters over again. For example, I applied these two delimiters I set up to a range of cells with the values 1 2 3 4 5 6 7 8 and the result was 1 2, 3 4, 5 6, 7 8 because it used the space, then the comma with a space and then started over at the start again with the space followed by the comma with a space.

(Maybe that's only interesting to me. But this is a new-to-me function so I like to kick the tires a bit when I find a function I haven't used before.)

One more thought here. If you do end up using this function and have a situation where you have the potential for double spaces to appear (so maybe you said FALSE to ignoring empty cells and used a space as your delimiter, you can put the TRIM function, which we'll talk about next, around the entire function to remove those double spaces as you generate your results.

Something like this:

$$=TRIM(TEXTJOIN(\$A\$12:\$B\$12,0,A8:D8))$$

# The TRIM Function

**Notation:** TRIM(text)

**Excel Definition:** Removes all spaces from a text string except for single spaces between words.

The TRIM function can come in very handy if you're trying to clean up text entries that are messy like the ones we just discussed had the potential to be.

If I used TEXTJOIN to merge a list of names that had first name followed by a space followed by middle name followed by a space followed by last name and I didn't suppress blank entries I would very likely end up with a list of entries with extra spaces in it.

Because for every entry that didn't have a middle name there would be an unwanted space.

So I might have "Albert  Jones" as one of my entries. There's an extra space there between Albert and Jones because there was no middle name.

To remove those extra spaces, you can use the TRIM function. If that entry was in Cell B2, I'd just write

$$=TRIM(B2)$$

Done. My new entry would be "Albert Jones".

I could also do that in the entry itself as I mentioned above by putting the TEXTJOIN function inside the TRIM function.

$$=TRIM(TEXTJOIN(…))$$

where the ... represents the values for the TEXTJOIN function.

Just make sure that you have enough closing parens when you do something like that. One for each of the functions you used.

TRIM also works with text pasted directly into the function as long as you use quotation marks around the text. For example,

=TRIM("Albert  Jones ")

would return Albert Jones without the extra spaces.

Also, remember that when you use TRIM it's still a formula. To get just the text entry and not keep the formula you need to copy your data and then paste special – values when you're done. (That goes for TEXTJOIN above as well.)

You probably won't need to use TRIM often, but it's very useful when you do need it. Also, if you're pulling information off a website and have issues, see the TRIM Excel Help text for more guidance on how it can help with that.

# The TODAY Function

**Notation:** TODAY( )

**Excel Definition:** Returns the current date formatted as a date.

I wanted to include a date function in the top ten functions and the TODAY function is very simple and basic but useful at the same time.

If you need today's date formatted as a date, you just enter

$$=\text{TODAY}(\ )$$

into a cell or a formula and that's what you'll get. You need the empty parens after TODAY for it to work. (The space between the parens is not needed.)

Now, you might be asking yourself why you'd bother doing something like this. I mean, can't you just type in today's date? Yes, you can.

But the reason to use TODAY is because you are creating a worksheet that uses the current date, whatever that is, in a calculation. So let's say you want to track which of your customer invoices are past thirty days. In other words, who should've paid you by now.

You can have a cell in your worksheet that uses TODAY so that you never have to re-enter today's date when making your calculations. That cell will update each time you open your worksheet, and then you can combine that with a calculation that looks at date billed to calculate how many days past due someone is on their payment. That, too, will automatically update each time you open your worksheet.

It is possible to place TODAY directly in a calculation formula if you want. (But remember the best practice is to have all of your assumptions visible. If you bury TODAY in a formula and someone doesn't realize it they may believe the values are static when in fact they will change each day as that value updates.)

So Option 1 is to put =TODAY( ) into Cell A1, have the date of the invoice in Cell C3, and then have the formula =A1-C3 to calculate the difference.

(Be sure that you format the cell with the calculation in it as a number because otherwise it will default to a date format that will look like a date sometime around 1900. We'll discuss how Excel handles dates later when we talk about more date functions, but the basic gist is that every date in Excel is actually stored as a number.)

Option 2 is to put =TODAY( )-C3 into a cell where C3 is the date the customer was invoiced.

Both work.

If you wanted to put both dates directly in your calculation formula, you'd likely have to use the DATE function for the other date, which we'll discuss later in the Date & Time Functions section.

If the time of day matters you can use the NOW function instead since TODAY is set to include a time of midnight.

Okay. Now on to one of the most powerful functions that Excel has, in my opinion, the IFS function.

# The IFS Function

**Notation:** IFS(logical_test1, value_if_true1,…)

**Excel Definition:** Checks whether one or more conditions are met and returns a value corresponding to the first TRUE condition.

This is another function that was new with Excel 2019 and as far as I can tell can completely replace the IF function. But if you need backwards compatibility then you'll need to work with the IF function instead (which will be discussed briefly later).

The IF function was always one of my favorite functions, if such a thing can exist, so I'm certain that I will also love IFS.

IFS at its most basic lets you write a formula that says, "If X happens return Y, otherwise return Z." That's pretty simple. Powerful but simple.

But the reason I always loved the IF function was because I could nest them. So I could say, "If X happens, return Y. If X doesn't happen, but G does, then return H. And if neither X nor G happens, then return Z."

And I could keep going and going and going with that until I had twenty possible outcomes. I won't deny that it was very tricky to build a nested IF function. That's where my warnings about matching up your opening and closing parens come from, because if you don't it all turns to mush with nested IF functions.

But the beauty of IFS is that it is designed to make it easier to build a nested IF function. No more keeping track of a million closing parens.

Let's walk through some examples.

First we'll build a simple function to give free shipping to any customer who spends at least $25. Any customer who spends less than $25 will pay 5% in shipping costs.

To calculate our shipping cost, we write that as

=IFS(A1>=25,0,TRUE,A1*0.05)

Let's break that down.

The first part, the IF part of our first condition, is A1>=25. We're saying that if the customer's purchase in Cell A1 is greater than (>) OR equal to (=) 25 then we want the first outcome.

We then place that first outcome after the comma. In this case that's 0.

Which makes the THEN part of our first outcome 0. If the customer's purchase is equal to or greater than 25, then don't charge for shipping.

That leaves us with the third part, our ELSE portion of the decision tree.

Because this is the IFS function and we could list out ten of these conditions before we get to the end we have to put TRUE to tell Excel this is the closing condition, otherwise Excel won't know we're at the end.

So the next entry is TRUE and then there's a comma and then we have our calculation of the shipping cost when the transaction is for less than $25.

And that's

A1*0.05

Notice that for the calculation A1*.05 we don't have to use quotation marks. (Unlike some other functions where you do.)

Also note here that we are calculating the *shipping charge*, not the customer's transaction cost. If we wanted the total customer cost we would use A1*1.05 for that last section and A1 for the earlier value.

Okay. That was a basic IFS function. One condition, two possible outcomes.

The complexity level ratchets up when you start to nest conditions. Let's look at the basic format of an IFS function again.

It's IF-THEN-ELSE, right? IF x, THEN y, ELSE z.

Or IF-THEN-OTHERWISE. IF x, THEN y, OTHERWISE z.

When you start to add conditions using the IFS function it becomes a situation where you're saying, "If this, then that, but if it's not this but instead this other thing, then…but if it's not that other thing either but it is this thing over here, then…" and so on and so on and so on.

You can write an IFS function with 127 different conditions in it. (Although Excel and I both would not recommend doing so because the order in which you add your conditions is crucial and that would be really hard to get right.)

Confused yet? It sounds horribly complicated doesn't it?

# Top 10 Functions

Let's walk through an example which should help this come clear.

We're going to build an IFS function that calculates a customer discount that escalates as customers spend more and more money.

If a customer spends at least $25 they get $5 off. If they spend $75 they get $10 off. If they spend $100 they get $15 off. And if they spend $250 they get $25 off.

For me the easiest way to do this is to build a table of the values and discounts and work from there. Here it is with our discount table up top and our test values down below.

|   | A | B | C |
|---|---|---|---|
| 1 | Order Amount | Discount Amount | |
| 2 | $25.00 | $5.00 | |
| 3 | $75.00 | $10.00 | |
| 4 | $100.00 | $15.00 | |
| 5 | $250.00 | $25.00 | |
| 6 | | | |
| 7 | Customer Spend | Rebate | Formula in Column B |
| 8 | $10.25 | | |
| 9 | $27.50 | | |
| 10 | $74.95 | | |
| 11 | $100.00 | | |
| 12 | $225.00 | | |
| 13 | $250.00 | | |

We have the cut-off order amounts in Cells A2 through A5 and the discounts the customer will receive at each level in Cells B2 through B5.

Below that starting in Cell A8 are the values we're going to use to test our discount formula.

Let's start building our function. Our first condition is that if they spend under $25 they receive no discount.

We write that as

$$=\text{IFS}(A8<A2,0$$

The next condition is that if they spend less than $75 (the value in Cell A3) but at least $25 (which we've already determined is true with the first part of the function) they will get $5 off (the value in Cell B2).

Let's add that to our formula:

=IFS(A8<A2,0,A8<A3,B2

(Note that because of the way I built my table the order amount and the discount amount are pulling from different rows in this example.)

From this point onward we just keep adding each layer of discount until we've added all but the last one:

=IFS(A8<A2,0,A8<A3,B2,**A8<A4,B3,A8<A5,B4,**

At which point we add our final closing condition which is going to be TRUE,B5 and we close it out with a closing paren.

Adding in $ signs to fix our table reference so that we can copy this formula down to the rest of the cells we end up with:

=IFS(A8<$A$2,0,A8<$A$3,$B$2,A8<$A$4,$B$3,A8<$A$5,$B$4, TRUE,$B$5)

That looks like a complex mess, but it's actually simpler than the same formula using an IF function because with an IF function we would have had to insert an IF between every change in condition and made sure that all our closing parens were in the right place. Here we just have one function to do the same thing.

Here are our results and the formula for each row.

| 7 | Customer Spend | Rebate | Formula in Column B |
|---|---|---|---|
| 8 | $10.25 | $0.00 | =IFS(A8<$A$2,0,A8<$A$3,$B$2,A8<$A$4,$B$3,A8<$A$5,$B$4,TRUE,$B$5) |
| 9 | $27.50 | $5.00 | =IFS(A9<$A$2,0,A9<$A$3,$B$2,A9<$A$4,$B$3,A9<$A$5,$B$4,TRUE,$B$5) |
| 10 | $74.95 | $5.00 | =IFS(A10<$A$2,0,A10<$A$3,$B$2,A10<$A$4,$B$3,A10<$A$5,$B$4,TRUE,$B$5) |
| 11 | $100.00 | $15.00 | =IFS(A11<$A$2,0,A11<$A$3,$B$2,A11<$A$4,$B$3,A11<$A$5,$B$4,TRUE,$B$5) |
| 12 | $225.00 | $15.00 | =IFS(A12<$A$2,0,A12<$A$3,$B$2,A12<$A$4,$B$3,A12<$A$5,$B$4,TRUE,$B$5) |
| 13 | $250.00 | $25.00 | =IFS(A13<$A$2,0,A13<$A$3,$B$2,A13<$A$4,$B$3,A13<$A$5,$B$4,TRUE,$B$5) |

I only had to write the formula once because after I'd finished in Cell B8 and the $ signs were in place, I could just copy and paste down to the other cells.

Note that the A8 references in the above formula did not get $ signs because that's the cell reference that needs to change with each row. But all the others did because they needed to be fixed references.

Also, always remember with an IFS function to check the edge cases. In this instance that's values of $25, $75, $100, and $250, to make sure that they are falling into the correct category.

The way I just showed you is one way to write that function to get the result we needed, but I could have just as easily written it using greater than and equals to instead.

Let's do that now for just the first two conditions, a discount of $5 at $25 and a discount of $10 at $75. In this case we have to start with the highest discount first to get it to work.

So our first condition is if the customer spend (in Cell A8) is greater than or equal to our highest order level ($75 in Cell A3) then they will get our highest discount ($10 in Cell B3):

=IFS(A8>=A3,B3

If that's not true, then if the spend is greater than our next level spend cutoff (in this case $25 in Cell A2) then they will get our next level discount (in this case $5 in Cell B2):

=IFS(A8>=A3,B3,A8>=A2,B2,

And if that's not true either then we're out of discounts and we close it off with TRUE and a discount of zero.

=IFS(A8>=A3,B3,A8>=A2,B2,TRUE,0)

Note how in this version the customer spend and discount amount were pulled from the same row for each discount level.

Okay.

Don't get upset if you write one of these wrong the first time, I usually do. I did on this last one. Because it was easier for me to mentally build from the lowest level up like we did the first time rather than start on the highest level and work my way down like we had to on this one.

I just keep faith that this is all logic, pure and simple, and that if something isn't working the way it should it's because I haven't mapped out the steps properly and I just need to keep trying until I figure out where I went wrong.

If you really, really get stuck, pull out a piece of paper and starting drawing one of those branching decision trees. You know, "we started here, branch one is this, it got us here, branch two is this, it gets us there," etc. until you've drawn out the whole thing.

For example, with the function we just wrote: We started with any purchase amount. If that amount was greater than or equal to $75 that's our first branch and it took us to a discount of $10. But if it wasn't $75 or more then we take the other branch Okay. Now what? What happens down that branch? If it's equal to or more than $25 then we go down a branch that takes us to a discount of $5. But if that branch isn't true, where does that take us? To a discount of zero.

It's a little bit of mental gymnastics. Some take to it better than others. But if you can master it, I personally think the IFS function and its related functions (COUNTIFS, SUMIFS, etc.) are some of the most useful functions in Excel.

Okay. On to something simpler. The AND function.

## The AND Function

**Notation:** AND(logical1, [logical2],…)

**Excel Definition:** Checks whether all arguments are TRUE, and returns TRUE if all arguments are TRUE.

I wanted to include one logic function in this top ten list and the AND function is the one I probably use the most.

At its core, the AND function is very basic. You use it to determine whether more than one condition has been met. So, is that value greater than 10 AND less than 20? Is that customer from Alaska AND has he bought Widgets?

It doesn't have to be just two criteria either. You can use more than two with an AND function. (Although the help text for the function doesn't say exactly how many you can use.)

In my numeric example above, you would write that as

$$=AND(A1>10,A1<20)$$

If the value in Cell A1 was greater than 10 and less than 20 Excel would return a value of TRUE. Otherwise it would return a value of FALSE.

In the second example I gave, you could write that as

$$=AND(A1="Alaska",B1="Widget")$$

where Cell A1 contained the State and Cell B1 contained the Product.

Again, if both criteria were met, Excel would return a value of TRUE.

In addition to working with numbers, like the first example above, and text references, like the second example above, AND works with cell references. So:

$$=AND(A1>D1,A1<D2)$$

looks to see if the value in Cell A1 is greater than the value in Cell D1 and also less than the value in Cell D2.

I rarely if ever use AND on a standalone basis. You could, like I showed in the examples above, but what I've used it for instead was if I had an IF function where I needed two criteria met.

For example, if I wanted all customers who bought Widgets and live in Alaska to qualify for 50% off their purchase amount where the purchase amount is in Cell C1, I could write an equation to calculate total cost as:

$$=IFS(AND(A1="Alaska",B1="Widget"),C1*0.5,TRUE,C1)$$

Or, using the IF function which is simpler to write in this case:

$$=IF(AND(A1="Alaska",B1="Widget"),C1*0.5,C1)$$

Either of those options would take 50% off the purchase amount if both conditions were met. In this case, the IFS function is the more complex one because it needs that TRUE in there to complete the function. But you could create a nested function where you walk through multiple discounts, Alaska & Widgets, California & Whatchamacallits, etc. and then the IFS function would be the easier one to work with.

Okay. Let's close out our top ten with a function that many of my friends swear by and that I've come around on but am still not a hundred percent in love with, VLOOKUP.

# The VLOOKUP Function

**Notation:** VLOOKUP(lookup_value, table_array, col_index_num, [range_lookup])

**Excel Definition:** Looks for a value in the leftmost column of a table, and then returns a value in the same row from a column you specify. By default, the table must be sorted in an ascending order.

As I just mentioned, I have friends who think that VLOOKUP is the best function in Excel. These are people whose jobs involve computers and databases and analysis, so they should know what they're talking about.

For me personally, it feels like every time I've wanted to use VLOOKUP it's caused me more problems than it's been worth. But that's because I'm always trying to use it after the fact. So my columns aren't in the right order or I forget that my data has to be sorted and it annoys me.

When I set out up front to use VLOOKUP and specifically build my table to work with it, I actually like it. If you've done that it's easier than building a series of nested IF functions. (Or working with IFS.)

So. To effectively use VLOOKUP you need a data table that has two things: one, values that can be looked up that are sorted in ascending order and, two, values in a column to the right of the first values that can be returned when a match is found.

A perfect use for VLOOKUP is something like the discount example above.

VLOOKUP can take each value, compare it to the purchase cutoffs in that discount table, and return a discount amount.

If you have a value that falls between two of the values in your reference table, for example, $10 is going to fall between $0 and $25, and you haven't told Excel to limit your results to exact matches, it will return the result that corresponds to the lower value. So, the one that corresponds to $0 in this example.

(This is why the sort on your table is so important when using VLOOKUP.)

So let's go ahead and pull the same values using VLOOKUP that we did using IFS.

The one adjustment we need to make to the table from above is we need to add a zero order amount row so that Excel has a value to pull for any input we give it that's below our first discount threshold of $25.

We can then quickly and easily write our VLOOKUP function. Here it is in the table and then we'll walk through what we're looking at:

|  | A | B | C |
|---|---|---|---|
| 1 | **Order Amount** | **Discount Amount** | |
| 2 | $0.00 | $0.00 | |
| 3 | $25.00 | $5.00 | |
| 4 | $75.00 | $10.00 | |
| 5 | $100.00 | $15.00 | |
| 6 | $250.00 | $25.00 | |
| 7 | | | |
| 8 | **Customer Spend** | **Rebate** | **Formula in Column B** |
| 9 | $10.00 | $0.00 | =VLOOKUP(A9,$A$1:$B$6,2) |
| 10 | $27.50 | $5.00 | =VLOOKUP(A10,$A$1:$B$6,2) |
| 11 | $74.95 | $5.00 | =VLOOKUP(A11,$A$1:$B$6,2) |
| 12 | $100.00 | $15.00 | =VLOOKUP(A12,$A$1:$B$6,2) |
| 13 | $225.00 | $15.00 | =VLOOKUP(A13,$A$1:$B$6,2) |
| 14 | $250.00 | $25.00 | =VLOOKUP(A14,$A$1:$B$6,2) |

The first input for VLOOKUP is the value from your data that you want to look up. So in the first row of our table that's going to be Cell A9.

$$=VLOOKUP(A9,$$

The next input for VLOOKUP is a reference to the cell range where Excel needs to look for that value and where the value you want it to return is also located.

The lookup value has to be in the left-hand column of your selected range.

If you have a twenty-column table and the value you want to look up is in the third column, then the range you enter here has to start with that third column and the value you're going to return has to be on the right-hand side of the lookup column.

In this case, we've built the table to work just fine with those constraints. We want to look up the value from Column A and return the value from Column B. (But that has tripped me up before, let me tell you.)

=VLOOKUP(A9,A1:B6,

The third entry in a VLOOKUP is which column in the range of cells you gave in the second entry contains the value you want to pull.

Given the constraints of VLOOKUP the first column contains what you're using for your search. Count from there to find your column number for your result.

In this example, our number is 2 because discount is in the second column in our range.

If you don't need exact matches, you're done. You can close it out with the last paren and hit enter.

Here's our final formula with $ signs added to fix the reference table range:

=VLOOKUP(A9,$A$1:$B$6,2)

What I left off of the formula above is a final, optional input, that tells Excel whether it's looking for an exact match (0/FALSE) or an approximate match (1/TRUE).

If it's an exact match, you'll only get a value returned when what you're looking up matches an entry in the table exactly.

If it's an approximate match you'll get a result for all entries and your value will be determined based on the table sort and where that value falls in the range of values.

Obviously the VLOOKUP I just used for our discount table is a lot simpler than the IFS equivalent we discussed earlier.

But as I said above, I run into issues using VLOOKUP because I want to use it on unsorted data or on data that has the value I want to pull to the left of the lookup value in my table. So for me personally it's easier to write an IFS function with a lot of inputs than it is to rearrange my data.

Just think of nested IF functions as the way to do VLOOKUP without all the pesky rules. But because there are no rules, you have to do a lot more of the heavy lifting up front.

A few more points:

Excel cautions that numbers or dates stored as text may produce unexpected results and so may text entries that have inconsistent usage of spaces or quote marks.

If the data table you're using for your lookup values is large or complex, be very, very careful that the results you get are what you expect. And absolutely be sure to sort your data table in ascending order.

Also check, double-check, and check again.

And one final point.

With an IF function to change the IF formula to adjust for whether you want your criteria to be "a customer spent $25 or more" versus "a customer spent over $25" you adjust the formula from >= to >. With VLOOKUP, you'll need to adjust your *lookup table* not your formula. So instead of $25.00 in the table, we'd have $25.01 for a situation where customers get the discount if they spend over $25 as opposed to $25 or more.

Okay. That's it for our top ten functions. On to Base Functions.

# Base Functions

The functions I'm putting in this category of "base functions", which is not a category that exists anywhere except right here, are those statistical or mathematical functions that are used as the base for the other IFS functions. Functions like COUNTIFS, SUMIFS, etc. We already covered SUM, but now we're going to cover the functions that let you take an average, count the number of values you have, take a minimum value, or take a maximum value as well as their iterations.

First up, the AVERAGE function.

# The AVERAGE Function

**Notation:** AVERAGE(number1, [number2],...)

**Excel Definition:** Returns the average (arithmetic mean) of its arguments, which can be numbers or names, arrays, or references that contain numbers.

AVERAGE is listed as a Statistical function by Excel, but when I think about taking an average I generally think of it along with addition and division. I add up my values and then divide by how many there are.

Also, the definition above is slightly confusing when I read it, so I'm going to rewrite it to clarify.

Let's write it as this: The AVERAGE function returns the average (arithmetic mean) of its arguments. The arguments can be numbers like 1, 2, 3, or 4. Or the arguments can be a named range, an array, or a cell reference as long as the cells or range referenced include numbers.

(If you try to apply AVERAGE to a range of cells with just text in them the result you get is the #DIV/0! error message.)

What the AVERAGE function does is it takes the sum of a range of numbers and then divides that sum by the number of entries in the range that had a numeric value.

For example, if I have the values 1, 2, 3, 4, and 5 in a range of 5 cells from A1 through A5 and I write

$$=AVERAGE(A1:A5)$$

Excel will add those values to get 15, divide that total by 5, and return a value of 3.

## Base Functions

If I include Cell A6, a blank cell, in that range, and write it as =AVERAGE(A1:A6), I get the same result even though I now have six cells in my range, because AVERAGE only looks at those cells that have values in them.

Likewise, if I have the word "test" in Cell A6 I will still get a result of 3 because only five of the cells in my range had numeric values.

This is very important. Because it may not be what you wanted.

To fix this when you have a cell in your range that should be included but where the value is blank instead of zero, you need to put a zero in that cell or it will not be included in your calculation.

In our example above, putting a zero in Cell A6 changes our average to 2.5 from 3 because we're now dividing 15 by 6 instead of 5.

AVERAGE will, of course, also work on values that you enter directly in the formula. So

=AVERAGE(1,2,3,4,5)

would return a value of 3. (But doing this is not recommended, as discussed in the best practices chapter.)

# The AVERAGEA Function

**Notation:** AVERAGEA(value1, [value2],…)

**Excel Definition:** Returns the average (arithmetic mean) of its arguments, evaluating text and FALSE in arguments as 0; TRUE evaluates as 1. Arguments can be numbers, names, arrays, or references.

If you need to take an average from a range that has non-numeric values in it and you need those cells included when calculating the average, you can use AVERAGEA to do so. (It doesn't fix the issue of a blank value, but it does fix the issue of dealing with text entries.)

As it says in the definition, AVERAGEA treats text entries and FALSE values as having a value of 0 and TRUE values as having a value of 1 when calculating the arithmetic mean.

If it's important to include the cells that have text in them, use AVERAGEA. If you want to exclude those cells, use AVERAGE.

For example, if I have four cells and they have the numeric values 10 and 6 and then the text values "This" and "That" in them, AVERAGEA and AVERAGE will return different results.

AVERAGE returns a value of 8 because it adds the 10 and 6 and only divides by 2 ignoring the cells that had text in them.

AVERAGEA returns a value of 4 because it adds the 10 and 6 plus zero for the cell with "this" in it and zero for the cell with "that" in it and then divides by 4.

Another interesting use for AVERAGEA is that because it assigns a value of 1 to TRUE outcomes and a value of 0 to FALSE outcomes, you can use it with the logical arguments like AND and OR or the IFS function to determine the average outcome of a scenario.

# Base Functions

For example, if I want to know what percent of the time my customers are both from Alaska and buy Widgets, I could use AVERAGEA in connection with an IF function. (I could do the same with COUNTIFS, but for now we're just going to look at IF and AVERAGEA for this.)

There are two formulas I'd need. The first, assuming the State is in Column A and the Product is in Column B, assigns TRUE or FALSE to each row depending on whether the result is Alaska and Widgets or some other combination.

=IF(AND(A2="Alaska",B2="Widgets"),TRUE,FALSE)

The second uses AVERAGEA to come up with an average value for those results using the TRUE and FALSE values. Assuming they're in Column C and Rows 2 through 8:

=AVERAGEA(C2:C8)

Note that the AVERAGEA function here has to start in the second row (Cell C2) because otherwise it would include the header row in its calculation since it counts text entries.

In my sample worksheet my result of that second formula was .28574 which meant that approximately 29% of the time the entries in Rows 2 through 8 were for customers who were both in Alaska and bought Widgets.

One thing to be careful of if you're going to try to use AVERAGEA in conjunction with TRUE/FALSE statements to get a percentage result:

I initially tried an iteration of this where it was Alaska & Widgets TRUE, Alaska FALSE, and then all other entries blank to try to get the percent of Alaskan customers who bought Widgets, but AVERAGEA wanted to count those blank results and I wasn't able to find a simple workaround for it using the IF function and AVERAGEA.

(Even if you have a blank cell sometimes Excel doesn't think you do. To find out whether it truly thinks a cell is blank and therefore worth ignoring, you can use the ISBLANK function in reference to a cell and see if you get back a TRUE or FALSE result.)

I even tried copy and paste special-values to remove the formula itself and Excel still insisted that those cells had a value in them even though they were completely blank.

This is a good reminder to check your results and make sure the value you're getting back makes sense. Also, if you can't accomplish a task with one approach, there may well be another. Don't get stuck on one solution if it isn't working.

## The COUNT Function

**Notation:** COUNT(value1, [value2],…)

**Excel Definition:** Counts the number of cells in a range that contain numbers.

The COUNT function is a very basic function. What COUNT does is it allows you to count how many cells within your specified range contain a number or a date.

(It basically gives you the number that AVERAGE uses to divide its results. And, yes, that does mean that AVERAGE will include a date in a range as part of its average.)

For example, a range of three cells that contain the values 1, 12/31/10, and "one" will be counted as 2 because the first two entries (1 and 12/13/10) are considered numbers, but the last entry ("one") is not.

If you have a cell that shows a numeric value due to a formula, so the cell contents are actually =SUM(2,3) but the cell displays 5, that will be counted as well.

Excel will also count a numeric value (1) that is formatted as text.

Also, for a cell to be counted it can only contain a number or date. For example, "1 day" would not be counted since it includes the number 1 but also the text "day".

The COUNT function itself is very simple to use. For example,

$$=COUNT(A1:A5)$$

will count the number of cells in the range from Cell A1 through Cell A5 that contain a number or date.

You could also write a function such as =COUNT(1,2,3) and it would count the number of numbers or dates in the list within the parens. In this case, three.

# Base Functions

If you don't want to limit your count to just numbers and dates, then you need to use COUNTA. The COUNTA function allows you to count how many cells within your specified range are not empty. So not just those that contain dates and numbers, but those that contain anything.

Be careful, however, because COUNTA will also count any cell that has a function in it even if that function is not currently displaying a value. (And using copy and then paste special – values to replace that function may not clear the cell enough for COUNTA to ignore it. You have to make sure that a cell is truly blank for it to not be counted.)

There is also a function, COUNTBLANK, which counts empty cells, but be sure to test it with your data since there is some overlap between what COUNTA and COUNTBLANK will count. Both count cells with "" in them.

## The MIN Function

**Notation:** MIN(number1, [number2],…)

**Excel Definition:** Returns the smallest number in a set of values. Ignores logical values and text.

Another useful Statistical function is the MIN function. This one takes a range of values or list of numbers and returns the smallest value.

You could say

$$=MIN(1,2,3)$$

and it would return a value of 1 or

$$=MIN(-1,0,1)$$

and it would return a value of -1, but the real power of this function is when you use it on a range of cells.

So, for example, let's say you want to know the lowest test score from a class that had 125 students in it and where all of the test scores were recorded in Column C. You would simply write the function as

$$=MIN(C:C)$$

and it would return for you the lowest test score in the range.

According to Excel, if you reference a range and ask Excel to return the minimum value and there are no numbers in the range it will return a value of zero.

# Base Functions

Also, if the range contains an error value such as #DIV/0! the function will return that error value. In this case, #DIV/0!

If there are dates in the range it will use those as well. Most current dates fall in the range of about 40,000-50,000 so that will only be relevant if your minimum values lie within that range.

But that does also mean that MIN can be used to pull the oldest date from a range of values. (Just remember to format the result as a date if you do that.)

The function MINA is much like MIN except that it will consider logical values and text in determining the minimum value. If you have a range that has TRUE and FALSE values in it, TRUE will be treated as a 1 and FALSE will be treated as a zero. Basic text entries such as "try" are also treated as zeros.

## The MAX Function

**Notation:** MAX(number1, [number2],…)

**Excel Definition:** Returns the largest value in a set of values. Ignores logical values and text.

MAX is the counterpart to MIN. Where MIN looks for the smallest value in the range, MAX looks for the largest value in the range.

So =MAX(1,2,3) will return a value of 3 because that's the largest number in the list of provided values. Once again, though, the optimal use of MAX is by applying it to a cell range, such as an entire column or row.

$$=MAX(4:4)$$

would return the maximum value in Row 4 of your worksheet, for example.

If there are no numbers in the specified range, MAX will return a value of 0.

If there is a cell that has an error message within the range, MAX will return that error message.

MAX ignores text entries and does not include logical values like TRUE or FALSE in its determination.

As with MIN, MAX will also work with dates. It will return the latest date in the series but formatted as a number so you have to change the formatting.

Also, just like with MIN and MINA, MAX has a counterpart, MAXA, which will incorporate logical values into its determination. TRUE values are treated as a 1 and FALSE values are treated as a 0. Also, text entries are treated as zeros.

# Logical* Functions

Now let us cover Logical Functions like the AND function we already discussed.

I have that little asterisk there because I'm also including one function, NA, in this section that Excel places in the Information category instead. But I think these five functions all fit together and are good to review before we cover the rest of what I think of as the IF-related functions.

# The OR Function

**Notation:** OR(logical1, [logical2],…)

**Excel Definition:** Checks whether any of the arguments are TRUE, and returns TRUE or FALSE. Returns FALSE only if all arguments are FALSE.

The OR function is similar to the AND function except it doesn't require that all of the conditions are met to return a TRUE value. With OR if one of the conditions in the list is met, then the value is TRUE.

Say, for example, I want to identify all of my customers who are in the states of Florida, Georgia, and North Carolina because I have a special promotion running in those states. I could write that as

=OR(A1="Florida",A1="Georgia",A1="North Carolina")

and if the value in Cell A1 is any of those (Florida, Georgia, or North Carolina), Excel would return a value of TRUE.

If none of the conditions were met, Excel would return a value of FALSE.

(Very random side comment to make, but important: Hopefully when you're reading this book the quote marks you see used in the formulas are what are called straight quotes. Meaning they have no curl to them, they are straight up and down. The default in Word and other programs is to turn quote marks into what are called smart quotes which curl around the text they're quoting. If you ever copy a formula from somewhere like Word into Excel and it has smart quotes instead of straight quotes, that formula will not work until you replace those smart quotes with straight quotes. So just be advised that can be an issue at times. I've run into it with Excel as well as with SQL.)

## Logical* Functions

Okay. Back to the OR function. This is one I rarely use as a standalone, but it is nice to use it with an IF function. So say I was running a 50% off price promotion in those three states, I could write an IF function that says,

=IF(OR(A1="Florida",A1="Georgia",A1="North Carolina"),C1*.5,C1)

or an IFS function that says

=IFS(OR(A1="Florida",A1="Georgia",A1="North Carolina"),C1*0.5,
TRUE,C1)

to give a 50% discount to any customer in one of those three states.

Like with AND, you can use text criteria (like above), numeric criteria, or cell references. So

=OR(A1=C1,A1=C3)

would check to see if the value in Cell A1 was the same as the value in Cell C1 OR the value in Cell C3. And

=OR(A1=5,A1=10)

would check to see if the value in Cell A1 was equal to 5 OR 10.

# The TRUE Function

**Notation:** TRUE( )

**Excel Definition:** Returns the logical value TRUE.

When I was working on this guide I found myself occasionally needing a cell to return a value of TRUE or FALSE to test some of the different functions. Simply typing TRUE into the cell didn't always work, so I found myself using TRUE and its counterpart, FALSE.

If you use it, be sure to include the parens ( ) or Excel may think you're trying to reference a named range. (It works with a space between the parens like I have here or without a space between them.)

You should also be able to just type TRUE and get the same result, but that didn't always seem to work for me.

According to Excel, TRUE and FALSE exist primarily for compatibility with other spreadsheet programs. FALSE is just like TRUE except you type =FALSE( ) instead.

# The NA Function

**Notation:** NA( )

**Excel Definition:** Returns the error value #N/A (value not available)

You can use the NA function to mark empty cells. This avoids the issue of inadvertently including empty cells in your calculations.

A friend of mine suggested including it in this guide because he recently had a scenario where he was generating results using an IF function and then graphing those results. When his results generated an empty cell or a null value Excel tried to include those entries in the graph. He found that using NA fixed that problem, because Excel does not graph #N/A values.

To do this, you could write something like:

$$=IF(A1>10,5,NA(\ ))$$

In this case, if A1 is greater than 10, Excel returns a value of 5 but if it isn't Excel returns a value of #N/A.

Be sure to use the empty parens as I did in the example above or Excel won't recognize it as the NA function.

Also, be careful using this one because it will make some calculations return a value of #N/A.

# The NOT Function

**Notation:** NOT(logical)

**Excel Definition:** Changes FALSE to TRUE, or TRUE to FALSE.

This next one, the NOT function, is one I'm including only because Microsoft themselves highlight it as useful.

Also, it is related to the AND and OR functions. But the fact of the matter is that my psychology background tells me that using a negative to build a function is a bad idea and I would encourage you to find another way to accomplish your goal if you're ever tempted to use the NOT function.

At its most basic, the NOT function returns the opposite result. So

$$=\text{NOT(FALSE)}$$

returns a value of TRUE. And

$$=\text{NOT(TRUE)}$$

returns a value of FALSE.

But you're never going to use it that way.

Where you might want to use it is to evaluate whether your criteria were met.

So let's say that I have two conditions that must be met for someone to be given a bonus. They have to have been employed for over 12 months and they have to have generated over $25,000 in sales.

I could use a NOT function to ask if that happened. So, for the first criteria, was my employee's time with the company in Cell B5 greater than 12 months?

# Logical* Functions

To do this with a not function, I'd write

$$=NOT(B5<12)$$

to get a result of FALSE when the employee had not been there at least 12 months and a result of TRUE if they had.

See how I had to do less than 12 there to get the right result?

I could have just as easily used an IF function instead and written

$$=IF(B5>12,TRUE)$$

to get the same result without the mental gymnastics using the NOT function requires.

In the Excel help text for this function, they give their own bonus scenario and then write a really ugly looking formula to calculate the bonus. It looks like this:

$$=IF(AND(NOT(B14<\$B\$7),NOT(C14<\$B\$5)),B14*\$B\$8,0)$$

But let me flip that around for you by removing the NOT function and switching the less than signs to greater than signs. If I do that I get:

$$=IF(AND(B14>=\$B\$7,C14>=\$B\$5),B14*\$B\$8,0)$$

It returns the same result as using the NOT function but with a lot less headache. (Just be sure to test that border case of equals to B7 and B5 to make sure you get it exactly right…I had initially written it as > instead of >=, a common problem I have to watch out for.)

Bottom line with the NOT function: If you're ever tempted to use it ask yourself if there isn't a different and simpler way to do what you're trying to do. I'm not going to say that there's absolutely no possible use for this function, but I am pretty confident in saying that ninety-nine times out of a hundred you should be able to find an alternate way of doing your calculation that doesn't require you to use the NOT function.

But for that remaining one in a hundred scenario, now you know how to use it.

# IF Functions

Alright. Now we're back to a powerful set of functions, what I refer to collectively as the IF Functions.

We needed the base math functions and the logical functions that we just discussed as tools to help with understanding and working with these more advanced IF functions, but the functions we're about to discuss are ten times more powerful in my opinion than any of what we just covered.

In Excel 2019, Excel introduced MINIFS and MAXIFS to what it already had, which was SUMIFS, AVERAGEIFS, and COUNTIFS. About all they're missing at this point is MEANIFS and MEDIANIFS.

SUMIFS, AVERAGEIFS, and COUNTIFS are upgraded versions of SUMIF, AVERAGEIF, and COUNTIF that can be used in place of those earlier functions.

There never was a MINIF or MAXIF.

The reason I bring this up is because of backwards compatibility. Do not do what I did which is when SUMIF came out use it in a complex worksheet that your client then can't use because they're still on an old version of Excel.

Be sure before you use these highly valuable functions that you can use them in the setting you need to use them in. If not, you can recreate what they do with the underlying function and nested IF functions and maybe a cascading series of steps.

I'm not going to walk through that here, though, because this book is about Excel 2019. So I am going to assume that you are only working in Excel 2019 or with others who are also working in Excel 2019 or newer versions and so have full access to these functions.

I'm also not going to cover SUMIF, AVERAGEIF, or COUNTIF because their "plural" cousins can do everything they can. (I did cover them in *50 Useful Excel Functions* if that's really an issue. Also, Excel's help function is great. The principle for how they work is the same, but each one is limited to just one IF condition and the order of the inputs is likely different.)

Okay. Now that we have that out of the way. At a very high level what these functions do is they perform a calculation (SUM, AVERAGE, COUNT, MIN, or MAX) on a range of values when a set of criteria have been met.

So they only SUM when the customer is from Alaska and bought Widgets. Or they only take the MIN value when the transaction occurred after January 1, 2020.

Essentially they combine IF and the underlying function into one nice little bundle.

That's the bulk of what we're about to walk through in this section. I have also included the basic IF function as well as IFNA and IFERROR, the latter two of which let you suppress ugly error messages in your results.

Alright? Let's dive in with IF.

# The IF Function

**Notation:** IF(logical_test, [value_if_true], [value_if_false])

**Excel Definition:** Checks whether a condition is met, and returns one value if TRUE, and another value if FALSE.

We're not going to spend a lot of time on the IF function in this book because the IFS function should be able to replace it and if you're new to Excel I encourage you to learn the IFS function instead.

But I'm so grounded in using the IF function and other people you work with may be as well, that it deserves a quick pass.

So the IF function at its most basic lets you set up an IF-THEN-ELSE or IF-THEN-OTHERWISE set of conditions just like the IFS function did.

A basic IF function requires less inputs than the basic IFS function. Let's take the shipping example we used for IFS

$$=IFS(A1>=25,0,TRUE,A1*0.05)$$

That was saying that if the value in A1 is greater than or equal to 25, our shipping cost should be zero, otherwise it should be 5% of the value in A1.

With IF that same formula is:

$$=IF(A1>=25,0, A1*0.05)$$

We don't need that extra TRUE in there to tell Excel this is the last condition. But where IFS shines compared to IF is in the more complex nested functions.

Let's take that final sample from IFS that we used:

$$=IFS(A8>=A3,B3,A8>=A2,B2,TRUE,0)$$

That was saying that if the value in Cell A8 is greater than or equal to the value in Cell A3 then return a value of B3. ELSE if the value in A8 is greater than or equal to A2 return a value of B2. OTHERWISE return a value of 0.

I wrote that with the ELSE and the OTHERWISE in the descriptions because every time it's an ELSE if you're working with a basic IF function you need to put in a new IF function in your formula. Like so:

$$=IF(A8>=A3,B3,IF(A8>=A2,B2,0))$$

See that I have two IF functions in there? And that I had to close it out with two closing parens, one to close the first IF function and one to close the second IF function?

Okay. So those are some simple examples of IF versus IFS. If you're new to Excel just learn IFS.

But if you do enough in Excel you may run into a very complex IF function written by someone like me who has used them for years. And if you need to troubleshoot that function I want to give you a few tips on how to approach that.

Here's an incredibly complex nested IF function:

$$=IF(A22>\$A\$2,IF(A22>\$A\$3,IF(A22>\$A\$4,$$
$$IF(A22>\$A\$5,IF(A22>\$A\$5,\$B\$5),\$B\$4),\$B\$3),\$B\$2),0)$$

(This is an example written in what I find the harder format for nested IF functions because each new IF function is added in the middle of the formula rather than the end which makes it much harder to see where each IF function actually starts and ends..)

What I do if I have to troubleshoot a mess like this is remove everything except the first IF function. So I take that mess up there and I make it:

$$=IF(A22>\$A\$2,"THEN\ X",0)$$

Everything in the middle is irrelevant until I make sure that the first part works. If it does, then I drop that part of the formula away and check the next part with everything that isn't part of *that* IF function removed.:

$$=IF(A22>\$A\$3,"THEN\ X",\$B\$2)$$

# IF Functions

And so on and so on until I've found the part that was written incorrectly Does that make sense?

Remember when working with nested IF functions: slow and steady wins the race. Take it one step at a time. Test your possible outcomes. Don't get frustrated. Draw a diagram if you have to.

Okay, now on to COUNTIFS.

## The COUNTIFS Function

**Notation:** COUNTIFS(criteria_range1, criteria1, [criteria_range2, criteria2],…)

**Excel Definition:** Counts the number of cells specified by a given set of conditions or criteria.

COUNTIFS will count the number of times your conditions are met in a selected range of cells. It does not have a calculation range like SUMIFS, AVERAGEIFS, etc. that we're going to discuss after this, because there's nothing to perform a calculation on. It's just counting how many times your conditions are met in the specified range of cells.

If you set more than one condition, the criteria ranges for all of the conditions must be the same size. To set just one condition only provide one criteria range and criteria.

You may run into COUNTIF in older versions of Excel or when only one condition is being used, but with COUNTIF and COUNTIFS the order of the inputs are identical so that shouldn't trip you up.

If you reference multiple conditions, your criteria do not have to be of the same type. Criteria can use numeric values (24 or "24"), cell references (A1), expressions (">42"), or text ("how").

Cell references and numbers do not need to be in quotation marks, but expressions and text references do.

For example:

$$=COUNTIFS(A1:A5,B2)$$

# IF Functions

says to count how many times the values in Cells A1 through A5 are the same as the value in Cell B2.

$$=COUNTIFS(A1:A5,"YES")$$

says to count how many times the values in Cells A1 through A5 are the text YES. It will only count those instances where the full value in the cell matches the value given in the quotes. So a cell that says YES, PLEASE would not be counted. Nor would one that has YES followed by an extra space. It has to be an exact match unless you use wildcards, which we'll cover in a moment.

$$=COUNTIFS(A1:A5,">20")$$

says to count how many cells between Cell A1 and Cell A5 have a numeric value greater than 20. Note that even though the criteria is related to a number value that it's still shown in quotes because it's an expression. (If you had =COUNTIFS(A1:A5,20), which looks for any cells with a value equal to 20, you wouldn't need the quotes but you could still use them.)

If you want to reference a cell for your criteria but you also want to use a greater than or less than symbol, you need to combine the two using an ampersand (&).

For example

$$=COUNTIFS(A1:A5,">="\&G2)$$

would count how many times the cells in the range from Cell A1 to Cell A5 contain a value that is greater than or equal to the value in Cell G2.

You can also use wildcards with the COUNTIFS function if your condition relates to a text value.

The asterisk (*) represents any number of characters or spaces. If you simply wanted to count any cell that contains text you would write that as

$$=COUNTIFS(A1:A5,"*")$$

It can also be used in combination with other letters to, for example, count any entry where there is an e. You would write that as

$$=COUNTIFS(A1:A5,"*e*")$$

The asterisks on either side of the e say to look for any cells where there is an e anywhere. If it were just on one side or the other then Excel would only look for words that starts with an e (e*) or ended with an e (*e).

If you want to count entries of a certain text length you can use the question mark (?) as a wildcard. It represents one single character. So

$$=COUNTIFS(A1:A5,"???")$$

would count all cells in the range from Cell A1 through A5 where the entry is three letters or spaces long. (It doesn't work with numbers.)

If you actually need to find an asterisk or question mark you can do so by using the tilde (~) before the mark you need. So ~? or ~* will look for an actual question mark or an actual asterisk

Always test different scenarios to make sure the count is counting everything you want it to but also not more than you want it to. (And be sure you've covered all possible scenarios in your testing, a mistake I know I've made at least once.)

Those were instances that would all work with COUNTIF or COUNTIFS because there was only one condition that needed to be met. Let's walk through a couple of scenarios that use multiple criteria now.

To count based upon multiple criteria, you simply include additional ranges and additional criteria for each one.

When you do so, the criteria range for all of your conditions must be the same size. So if your first cell range is A1:B25, then your other cell ranges must also be two columns wide and 25 rows long.

Ranges do not have to be adjacent, but they do have to be the same size.

The way the count is performed is it looks at all first cells in each of the criteria ranges and sees if the criteria for the first cell in each range is met.

If so, that entry is counted. If not, it isn't. It then moves on to the second cell in each of the criteria ranges and checks to see if all of the second cells meet the specified criteria. And so on and so on.

Each time all of the criteria are met, Excel counts that as 1.

Let's walk through an example to see this in action. I've created a table that has columns for State and Total Purchases for six customers and I want to count how many of my customers are both in Alabama (AL) and spent $250 or more. State is in Column A, Total Purchases is in Column B. The data is in Rows 2 through 7 with the header row in Row 1.

The function we need is:

$$=COUNTIFS(A1:A7,"AL",B1:B7,">=250")$$

# IF Functions

Here it all is:

| | A | B | C | D |
|---|---|---|---|---|
| 1 | State | Total Purchases | | Customers From AL Who Spent At Least $250 |
| 2 | AL | $ 275.00 | | 3 |
| 3 | AL | $ 250.00 | | Cell D2: =COUNTIFS(A1:A7,"AL",B1:B7,">=250") |
| 4 | AZ | $ 110.00 | | |
| 5 | AL | $ 95.00 | | |
| 6 | AR | $ 250.00 | | |
| 7 | AL | $ 300.00 | | |

Our answer is 3 even though there were four potential purchases from AL and four purchases for $250 or more. Only three purchases met both conditions.

Let's break that down.

The first criteria range is A1 through A7. (We could have just as easily used A2 through A7 but it doesn't matter in this case if I include the header row since it won't meet my count criteria.) Those are the entries with our State values in them.

We told Excel we wanted to count any entry where the state is "AL".

The second criteria range is B1 through B7. That's our Total Purchases.

And we told Excel that for that range we wanted to count any time when a value was greater than or equal to $250. That's written as ">=250".

(Since this is a number and not a cell range we don't need the ampersand to combine the two.)

Excel then started with Cells A2 and B2 and determined whether both conditions were met. In this case, yes, so that first observation was counted. It continued onward like that to the end. Cells A5 and B5 only met one condition so were not counted. Same with Cells A6 and B6.

But Cells A3 and B3 as well as A7 and B7 did meet both conditions so were counted to give a total count of 3.

Remember, it's always a good idea to test your results against your data. So if I had a thousand rows of data I was using this formula on, I might write it to just cover ten rows first so I could test that it was working as expected before expanding to a sample size too big for me to judge easily. (Although with most of these you could use the filter options to filter your data to the same criteria you're using in your formula and then count, average, sum, etc. the results to double-check. That's another option.)

Okay. On to SUMIFS.

# The SUMIFS Function

**Notation:** SUMIFS(sum_range, criteria_range1, criteria1, [criteria_range2, criteria2],...)

**Excel Definition:** Adds the cells specified by a given set of conditions or criteria.

SUMIFS allows you to sum the values in a range when multiple conditions are met. It can also work with just one condition if you only provide one criteria and one criteria range.

The first input is the range of cells that contain the values you want to add together. The second input is the range of cells that contain the values for your first criteria. The third input is the criteria itself. And then you just keep adding range of cells and condition that needs to be met until you have all of your criteria.

(Be careful if you ever do need to work with SUMIF which was this function's precursor, because the inputs are provided in a different order in SUMIF versus SUMIFS and SUMIF had less restraints than SUMIFS does.)

You can enter up to 127 conditions that need to be met before your values will be summed.

When using SUMIFS your sum range and the criteria ranges you use need to be the same size. They do not need to be next to one other or in any specific order on the worksheet, but they do need to cover the same number of rows and columns each.

SUMIFS can use a number (22 or "22"), an expression ("<13"), a text-based condition ("YES"), or a cell reference (H1) for the sum criteria. For anything except a single number or a cell reference, be sure to use quotation marks around your criteria.

# IF Functions

You also don't have to use the same type of condition for each range. So you can use an expression for your first condition, a cell reference for your second, and a text-based condition for your third.

For text-based criteria, you can also use wildcards. The asterisk (*) represents any number of characters, the question mark (?) represents a single character, and the tilde (~) is used to distinguish when you're actually searching for an asterisk or question mark.

(See the COUNTIFS discussion for more detailed examples of all of the above.)

Here is a simple SUMIFS function with two conditions:

=SUMIFS(A1:A25,B1:B25,"USD",C1:C25,">10")

This would sum the values in Cells A1 through A25 if the value in the corresponding cells in Cells B1 through B25 contain "USD" and the values in Cells C1 through C25 are greater than 10. For Cell A1 it would look to Cells B1 and C1, for Cell A2 it would look to Cells B2 and C2, and so on and so on.

SUMIFS is one of the functions that I use the most.

For example, I use it in my budget worksheet to sum the amount I still owe on my bills each month.

I'll list all of my bills due for the month in Column A, whether I pay them with cash or with a credit card in Column B, the amount due in Column C, and I'll put an X when the bill is paid in Column D.

The SUMIFS formula I use is then:

=SUMIFS(C1:C10,B1:B10,"CASH",D1:D10,"")

That says sum the values in Column C if the values in Column B are "CASH" and Column D is blank. That lets me know how much cash I need in my bank account before those bills hit. As far as Excel is concerned Cash and CASH are the same. It is not case-sensitive.

The other place I use this is with my payables from publishing. I am usually owed money at any given time in about five different currencies and from about ten different sources. I have a worksheet where I sum the amount owed in each currency that I haven't yet been paid using a formula similar to the one above. In this case the formula for my USD payments is:

=SUMIFS(B$3:B$91,D$3:D$91,"USD",E$3:E$91,"")

This says to sum the values in Cells B3 through B91 if the values in Cells D3 through D91 are USD and the values in those cells in Column E are blank. I use Column E to check off when I receive a payment, so once payment is received that cell is no longer blank for that particular row.

I have a formula like this for each of the currencies I'm owed money in (CAD, AUD, INR, EUR, GBP, etc.) which is what the $ signs help with. This way I can just copy the formula to however many rows I need and all I have to update is the currency abbreviation.

Or even better yet, I can use a cell reference for that USD, say K2, and then when I copy the formula down it just references that same column but the new row so the currency abbreviation updates without any more effort from me.

=SUMIFS(B$3:B$91,D$3:D$91,K2,E$3:E$91,"")

That's just two examples of the power of SUMIFS. If you start to think about it, there are any number of places you can use it.

# The AVERAGEIFS Function

**Notation:** AVERAGEIFS(average_range, criteria_range1, criteria1, [criteria_range2, criteria2],…)

**Excel Definition:** Finds average (arithmetic mean) for the cells specified by a given set of conditions or criteria.

The AVERAGEIFS function works just like SUMIFS except it takes an *average* of the values when a specified criteria is met. And just like SUMIFS and SUMIF, the order of the inputs in AVERAGEIFS differs from the order of the inputs in AVERAGEIF, so keep that in mind if you ever run into AVERAGEIF.

The inputs for the function are the range of cells that contain the values you want to average followed by the range of cells for your first condition and then the first condition parameters. If you want to use multiple criteria you then list the next range of cells and the next condition and so on and so on up to a total of 127 times.

Your average range and criteria range(s) must all be the same size and shape.

Your criteria do not have to be of the same type and can reference numeric values (24 or "24"), cells (A1), expressions (">42"), or text ("how").

Cell references and numbers do not need to be in quotation marks, expressions and text references do.

As with SUMIFS and COUNTIFS, you can use wildcards for text-based criteria. See the COUNTIFS description for examples.

For a value to be included in the average calculation, all of the conditions you specify must be met.

Be careful with empty cells, blanks, or text values where numbers are expected as these may generate an error message rather than a calculation or may impact the calculation.

(See the Excel help screen for the function for a full listing of the errors and adjustments that Excel makes. Always check a formula against a small sample of data to make sure you're getting the result you want.)

AVERAGEIFS evaluates TRUE values as 1 and FALSE values as 0.

The function will not work if the values in the average_range cannot be translated into numbers.

An example of using AVERAGEIFS might be if you were looking at student grades and wanted to see average score across teacher name and student gender to identify potential gender bias and/or overall score bias across teachers.

To do this, I'm going to build a table that has Test Score in Column A, Teacher Name in Column B, and Gender in Column C. Next, I'll build a table that has F and M in the header row on either side of a listing of the teacher names.

Finally I can then use AVERAGEIFS to pull into the second table the average score for female (F) and male (M) students for each teacher.

Here it is:

|    | A     | B       | C      | D | E        | F     | G       | H     | I | J | K |
| -- | ----- | ------- | ------ | - | -------- | ----- | ------- | ----- | - | - | - |
| 1  | Score | Teacher | Gender |   |          |       |         |       |   |   |   |
| 2  | 50    | Smith   | F      |   |          |       |         |       |   |   |   |
| 3  | 49    | Barker  | M      |   |          | F     |         | M     |   |   |   |
| 4  | 68    | Vasquez | F      |   |          | 80.25 | Smith   | 84.50 |   |   |   |
| 5  | 75    | Smith   | M      |   |          | 90.00 | Barker  | 68.67 |   |   |   |
| 6  | 90    | Barker  | F      |   |          | 68.00 | Vasquez | 76.00 |   |   |   |
| 7  | 94    | Smith   | M      |   |          |       |         |       |   |   |   |
| 8  | 93    | Barker  | M      |   | Cell F4: | =AVERAGEIFS($A$1:$A$13,$B$1:$B$13,G4,$C$1:$C$13,$F$3) | | | | | |
| 9  | 91    | Smith   | F      |   | Cell H4: | =AVERAGEIFS($A$1:$A$13,$B$1:$B$13,G4,$C$1:$C$13,$H$3) | | | | | |
| 10 | 76    | Vasquez | M      |   |          |       |         |       |   |   |   |
| 11 | 82    | Smith   | F      |   |          |       |         |       |   |   |   |
| 12 | 64    | Barker  | M      |   |          |       |         |       |   |   |   |
| 13 | 98    | Smith   | F      |   |          |       |         |       |   |   |   |

By putting the F and M values in Cells F3 and H3 to match the values in the Gender column in Column C I was able to reference those values with my formula. Same with the teacher last names in Column G.

The formula used in Cell F4 (for female students of Teacher Smith) is:

=AVERAGEIFS($A$1:$A$13,$B$1:$B$13,$G4,$C$1:$C$13,$F$3)

What that's saying is, average the values in Cells A1 through A13 where the values in Cells B1 through B13 are equal to the teacher name in Cell G4 and the gender of the student listed in Cells C1 through C13 is equal to the value in Cell F3.

# IF Functions

By using the $ signs in the formula I can then copy the formula down to the other two rows in that table without making any other changes.

I did have to adjust the reference to $F$3 when I then copied the formula over to Column H for the male side and make that $H$3.

But by using $G4 I didn't have to adjust the reference to the teacher name when I copied it over.

Done. (Not statistically robust because we don't have enough data to really draw any sort of conclusion at all, but you can see how it could be interesting with enough data and really doesn't take all that much time to create.)

Don't forget, too, that AVERAGEIFS can be used with a single condition as well. So you could use it to calculate the average customer order amount for each state if you had a list of states, for example.

=AVERAGEIFS(A1:A1000,B1:B1000,"CO")

Would take the average of the values in Cells A1 through A1000 where the value in Column B was "CO".

(If you're ever trying to do a quick double-check of your values with AVERAGEIFS you can select the cells that it should be averaging and look on the bottom right side of your Excel screen and you should see values for Average, Count, and Sum for the selected cells. If Excel doesn't see your entries as numbers it will only show a count value.)

That's AVERAGEIFS, now on to MINIFS.

# The MINIFS Function

**Notation:** MINIFS(min_range, criteria_range1, criteria1, [criteria_range2, criteria2],…)

**Excel Definition:** Returns the minimum value among cells specified by a given set of conditions or criteria.

The MINIFS function is a new function in Excel 2019. It works just like COUNTIFS, SUMIFS, and AVERAGEIFS except its purpose is to return the minimum value in a range of cells.

The inputs into the function are similar to the other functions we already discussed. The first input is the range with the values where your minimum value will be found. The next input is the range for your first condition. The third input is the condition. And so on and so forth up to 127 conditions.

As with the other functions, your min_range and criteria ranges need to all be the same size.

Your criteria do not have to be of the same type and can reference numeric values (24 or "24"), cells (A1), expressions (">42"), or text ("how"). Cell references and numbers do not need to be in quotation marks, expressions and text references do. And you can use wildcards for text-based criteria.

See the COUNTIFS description for examples of the various criteria types and wildcards.

Also, be sure your ranges are properly aligned. In the help section for this one they show an example where the ranges are not aligned and the function still works anyway because the ranges are the same size.

Also, the function will return a value of zero if there are not matches to the conditions you set, so be careful on that one because I can see a scenario where you might think zero was a legitimate result and it turns out that the zero result

# IF Functions

was just because the formula was written wrong.

So when would you use this? Well, let's go back to our grades by teacher and gender example and apply MINIFS instead of AVERAGEIFS.

| | A | B | C | D | E | F | G | H |
|---|---|---|---|---|---|---|---|---|
| 1 | Score | Teacher | Gender | | | | | |
| 2 | 50 | Smith | F | | | | | |
| 3 | 49 | Barker | M | | | F | | M |
| 4 | 68 | Vasquez | F | | | 50.00 | Smith | 75.00 |
| 5 | 75 | Smith | M | | | 90.00 | Barker | 49.00 |
| 6 | 90 | Barker | F | | | 68.00 | Vasquez | 76.00 |
| 7 | 94 | Smith | M | | | | | |
| 8 | 93 | Barker | M | | Cell F4: | =MINIFS($A$2:$A$13,$B$2:$B$13,$G4,$C$2:$C$13,$F$3) | | |
| 9 | 91 | Smith | F | | Cell H4: | =MINIFS($A$2:$A$13,$B$2:$B$13,$G4,$C$2:$C$13,$H$3) | | |
| 10 | 76 | Vasquez | M | | | | | |
| 11 | 82 | Smith | F | | | | | |
| 12 | 64 | Barker | M | | | | | |
| 13 | 98 | Smith | F | | | | | |

The formula in Cell F4 becomes:

=MINIFS($A$2:$A$13,$B$2:$B$13,$G4,$C$2:$C$13,$F$3)

That's basically the same as the formula we used for AVERAGEIFS except we swapped out the function. What's interesting here is that we can see that for Barker, the minimum score for his female students is 90. That highlights a flaw in this data, which is that there is just one female student in Barker's class. And with Vasquez we can see that the averages and the minimums are the same as well and that's because there's only data for two students for Vasquez in the entire table, one male and one female.

Next we'll do the same for MAXIFS.

91

# The MAXIFS Function

**Notation:** MAXIFS(max_range, criteria_range1, criteria1, [criteria_range2, criteria2],…)

**Excel Definition:** Returns the maximum value among cells specified by a given set of conditions or criteria.

MAXIFS was another new function added to Excel 2019. It works just like MINIFS except that it returns the maximum value in the range that meets the specified conditions.

Everything that held true for SUMIFS, AVERAGEIFS, and MINIFS also holds true for MAXIFS. The max_range and criteria_ranges need to be the same size and should be aligned correctly. If you have more than one condition they don't need to be the same type. You can use wildcards with text conditions. Criteria can reference numeric values, cells, expressions, or text.

Here is an example of applying MAXIFS to that same range of student scores that we applied it to for AVERAGEIFS and MINIFS:

|   | E | F | G | H |
|---|---|---|---|---|
| 3 |   | F |   | M |
| 4 |   | 98.00 | Smith | 94.00 |
| 5 |   | 90.00 | Barker | 93.00 |
| 6 |   | 68.00 | Vasquez | 76.00 |
| 7 |   |   |   |   |
| 8 | Cell F4: | =MAXIFS($A$2:$A$13,$B$2:$B$13,$G4,$C$2:$C$13,$F$3) | | |
| 9 | Cell H4: | =MAXIFS($A$2:$A$13,$B$2:$B$13,$G4,$C$2:$C$13,$H$3) | | |

# IF Functions

The formula used in Cell F4 this time is:

=MAXIFS($A$2:$A$13,$B$2:$B$13,$G4,$C$2:$C$13,$F$3)

This time the values we see in the analysis table we built are the maximum scores for each gender for students in each teacher's class.

Again this serves to highlight the fact that for Barker there is only one female student and for Vasquez there is only one male and one female student.

This is noticeable when comparing the results across all three functions we've applied to the data.

In this table the Average column uses AVERAGEIFS, the Min column uses MINIFS, and the Max column uses MAXIFS. (And because of how I built the table I could just write each formula once and copy it down the rest of that column.)

| Teacher | M/F | Average | Min | Max |
|---------|-----|---------|-------|-------|
| Barker  | F   | 90.00   | 90.00 | 90.00 |
| Barker  | M   | 68.67   | 49.00 | 93.00 |
| Smith   | F   | 80.25   | 50.00 | 98.00 |
| Smith   | M   | 84.50   | 75.00 | 94.00 |
| Vasquez | F   | 68.00   | 68.00 | 68.00 |
| Vasquez | M   | 76.00   | 76.00 | 76.00 |

Again, not a large enough data set to say anything about, but if it were a large data set, this is an excellent and easy way to compare grades across gender and teacher. It could as easily be used for sales performance by salesperson by month, product performance, etc.

Once you master one of these advanced IF functions you see that they all work pretty much the same way and so you can pick whichever one best suits your needs and be comfortable using it.

Okay. On to a few more "IF" functions that are a little different and more for cleaning things up than anything else, IFNA and IFERROR.

# The IFNA Function

**Notation:** IFNA(value, value_if_na)

**Excel Definition:** Returns the value you specify if the expression resolves to #N/A, otherwise returns the result of the expression.

The IFNA function is one that I rarely use because I'm so comfortable with using IF functions that I just quickly write an IF function that does the same thing, which is to suppress that pesky #N/A result that sometimes occurs with IF functions.

The way IFNA works is that you tell it a function to perform and if the result of that function is the #N/A error then instead of returning that error you can specify what Excel returns instead.

(I say function here, but the Excel help text calls it an argument.)

The easiest way to show how this works is to walk you through an example.

Let's say I have a list of my books I've published and how much I've spent on ads for those books each month. I also have a list of how much I've earned for each book each month. And I decide I want to combine those two sets of information to calculate a profit/loss per month for each book.

I can use the TEXTJOIN function to create an entry for both data sets that combines month-year-title into one column and then use VLOOKUP to look up the amount I spent on ads for each title in each month and bring that into the sales worksheet.

But when VLOOKUP can't find an entry—so in months where I had book sales but no ad spend, for example—Excel returns a value of #N/A.

When that happens within a column of data you can no longer click on that column and see its summed value. This would prevent me from easily checking

# IF Functions

that I'd captured all of my ad costs.

But I can easily fix this issue using the IFNA function.

If my original formula was:

=VLOOKUP(D:D,'Advertising Spend By Series'!E:F,2,FALSE)

(That's saying look for the value in Column D of this worksheet in Column E of the Advertising Spend by Series worksheet and then pull the value from Column F, but only if the two values are an exact match.)

The revised formula using IFNA is:

=IFNA(VLOOKUP(D:D,'Advertising Spend By Series'!E:F,2,FALSE),0)

That looks complicated, but it's not. All I did is wrap the IFNA function around what I already had for VLOOKUP.

Replace the VLOOKUP portion with an X and you have:

=IFNA(X,0)

Basically, if there's a value for VLOOKUP to return then return that value, otherwise return a zero.

I chose to return a value of zero, but you could easily have it return a text statement instead.

If you are going to have it return text, be sure to use quotation marks around the text you want returned. So if I wanted "No Match" returned instead of a zero, I'd use:

=IFNA(VLOOKUP(D:D,'Advertising Spend By Series'!E:F,2,FALSE),"No Match")

If you don't want anything returned, so you just want an apparently blank cell, then leave that second argument blank. You'll still need to use the comma, so it should look like this:

=IFNA(VLOOKUP(D:D,'Advertising Spend By Series'!E:F,2,FALSE),)

That will return a value of "" in that cell instead of the #N/A error message.

And that's it. It looks a little complicated because we were working with a VLOOKUP function, but it's really very simple.

Just take the formula you already have that's giving you the #N/A results, type IFNA( between the equals sign and that first function, go to the end, add a comma, put in the result you want returned when there's an #N/A result (if any), and then add a closing paren. Done.

Just keep in mind, of course, that you will not see an #N/A result if you use this function, which could hide from you valuable information about your calculation or your data.

Also, it's particular to just that type of error. Other error messages, such as #DIV/0!, will still be displayed.

If you want to suppress all error messages, then you need to use IFERROR which we'll discuss next.

# The IFERROR Function

**Notation:** IFERROR(value, value_if_error)

**Excel Definition:** Returns value_if_error if expression is an error and the value of the expression itself otherwise.

The IFERROR function is just like the IFNA function except that it will return your specified value for any error message, not just the #N/A error message. Error messages suppressed by the function include: #N/A, #VALUE!, #REF!, #DIV/0!, #NUM!, #NAME?, and #NULL!

So be sure before you use it that you are okay with suppressing all of those error messages. For example, the #REF! error message usually will tell you when you've deleted a cell that was being referenced by a formula. That for me isn't something I would like to hide. If I've made that mistake, I want to know it.

But if you have a range of cells with a formula in them that's returning, for example, the #DIV/0! error because you're currently dividing by zero, which is an issue I've run into in some of my worksheets, this might be a good option.

Your other option is to use a simple IFS function instead.

For example, I might use

$$=IFS(P1=0,"",TRUE,J1/P1)$$

in one of my worksheets, because it returns a #DIV/0! error until P1 has a value and that annoys me. IFERROR would work the same in that situation. I could use

$$=IFERROR(J1/P1,)$$

instead. Note that I left the second argument, the value_if_error empty which will return a blank cell as long as dividing the value in Cell J1 by the value in Cell P1 produces an error message.

To do that I still had to include the comma, though.

My temptation in using either IFNA or IFERROR is to have them return zeroes or empty cells, but I would recommend that if you're using IFERROR in a crucial situation that you have it return a text entry instead so that you always know when there's an error message that's being suppressed. So

$$=IFERROR(J1/P1,"No Value")$$

is probably a better choice than

$$=IFERROR(J1/P1,)$$

because you will know for a fact that the formula generated an error message and won't think that the value in that cell calculated as zero.

Note above that I used quotes around the text I wanted to have Excel display in the place of my error message, just like I did with IFNA.

# Lookup Functions

Alright, so that was our IF functions. Now on to another set of functions that are potentially useful, the Lookup Functions.

A quick note: If you're feeling like this is all a bit of a struggle you might want to skip this section for now because functions like INDEX and MATCH fall into what I think of as an advanced intermediate category. It might help to go read about the rest of the math functions and the date functions first, which are very easy to use, and then come back to this section later when you're more grounded in working with functions overall.

But I put this section here because I think the Lookup Functions have the most potential after the top ten functions and the IF functions to provide value.

VLOOKUP, which we already covered, is probably the most celebrated of these functions, but there are others you can use, and if you master all of them you will save yourself tremendous amounts of effort.

So let's start with VLOOKUP's counterpart, HLOOKUP.

# The HLOOKUP Function

**Notation:** HLOOKUP(lookup_value, table_array, row_index_num, [range_lookup])

**Excel Definition:** Looks up a value in the top row of a table or array of values and returns the value in the same column from a row you specify.

HLOOKUP is basically the horizontal equivalent to VLOOKUP. Where VLOOKUP scans down a column to match your value and then pulls a result from another column in the row where the match was made, HLOOKUP scans across a row to match your value and then pulls a result from another row in that column where the match was made.

So it's a transposed version of VLOOKUP.

VLOOKUP is the much more popular of the two options because of how most people structure their data. But let's say I have a table of data with month across the top and vendor across the left-hand side and I want to extract how much was earned on a specific vendor in a specific month. I could do that using HLOOKUP.

Here's an example data table and result for looking up March and then pulling the fourth row of data which corresponds to ACX:

|   | A | B | C | D |
|---|---|---|---|---|
| 1 |   | January | February | March |
| 2 | Amazon | $100.00 | $107.00 | $114.49 |
| 3 | Createspace | $37.00 | $39.59 | $42.36 |
| 4 | ACX | $23.50 | $25.15 | $26.91 |
| 5 | Con Sales | $10.00 |   |   |
| 6 |   |   |   |   |
| 7 | March, ACX | $ 26.91 |   |   |
| 8 | Cell B7: | =HLOOKUP("March",B1:D5,4,FALSE) |   |   |

# Lookup Functions

The formula I used was:

=HLOOKUP("March",B1:D5,4,FALSE)

That's saying look for an exact match to the word March in my data table contained in Cells B1 through D5 and then return the result for the fourth row in the data table.

Let's break this down further.

The first entry in any HLOOKUP formula is going to be what you're looking up. This can be a numeric value, a text string, or a cell reference. In the example above, because I wanted to look up a specific text value, I had to use quotation marks.

With text entries, you can also use the wildcards that Excel has for text lookups. A question mark means any one character and an asterisk means any number of characters. So "*April" would search for any text string that has April at the end whereas "?April" would only search for any text string that has one character before ending in April.

The second input into the HLOOKUP function is where you're going to search. That's the table array. The first row of that table array is where what you're searching for needs to be. The table array then has to have the row with the values you want to return somewhere below the search row.

I used B1:D5 here but I could have as easily used A1:D5 for the cell range.

The third input is which row in your table to pull the result from.

If you provide a negative number, you'll get an error message. If you provide a value that is larger than the size of the range you specified, you will also get an error message.

A value of 1 that will return either the value you were looking up (for an exact match) or the closest possible value (for an approximate match), which can be especially useful if you're trying to find the closest result to a specific value.

The fourth input is TRUE or FALSE to tell Excel what type of search it's performing. With HLOOKUP (as with VLOOKUP), there are two options for what you're searching for. You can search for an exact match (FALSE) or you can search for an approximate match (TRUE).

If you choose to search for an approximate match, then your data in the lookup row needs to be sorted in ascending order for HLOOKUP to work properly. If you're looking for an exact match (like in the example above) then the order of the entries doesn't matter.

(You can sort data in a row using the Sort option in the Data tab by clicking on Options when the Sort dialogue box appears and choosing to sort from left to right.)

When looking up values Excel treats uppercase and lower case entries as the same. It is not case sensitive.

If Excel can't find a match for an exact match search you will get an #N/A result.

You will also get an #N/A error if you ask for an approximate match but the lookup value you specify is smaller than the smallest value in the table.

If you do get an error message, check your spelling, that your table range is correct, and that your row references are correct. If that all looks good, then you can look at the help function for HLOOKUP to see which error message you received and what that might mean.

Where VLOOKUP to me seems to be best used for looking up values in a table, like a discount table, I see HLOOKUP as most useful when you want to extract data from an existing summary table like in the example I gave above. But the two do operate on the same principles, so if you understand how to use one you should be able to use the other as well.

If you go to the Excel help for HLOOKUP or VLOOKUP you may be a little confused because at the top it suggests that you use XLOOKUP instead. But if you try to type XLOOKUP into your worksheet, you'll find that Excel doesn't act like that's a function. That's because XLOOKUP is not actually available in Excel 2019. It's currently only available in Microsoft 365. And if like me you like to own your software after a one-time fee and not be someone's guinea pig, then you don't have Microsoft 365 so that little comment they put there is a bit of a moot point.

But know that some day in a future version of Excel there will likely be a function you can use called XLOOKUP that is a better version of HLOOKUP and VLOOKUP because it works in any direction and returns exact matches by default. Won't that be nice to have someday? But not today, at least not in Excel 2019.

# The SWITCH Function

**Notation:** SWITCH(expression, value1, result 1, [default_or_value2, result2],…)

**Excel Definition:** Evaluates an expression against a list of values and returns the result corresponding to the first matching value. If there is no match, an optional default value is returned.

In the meantime, we do have the SWITCH function which was added to Excel 2019. From what I can tell looking at the examples they give it allows you to make a calculation and then provide one of up to 126 different answers based on the result.

The examples that Excel provides for how to use this function are about providing the day of the week for a specific date. But the TEXT function does that better. They use:

=SWITCH(WEEKDAY(A2),1,"Sunday",2,"Monday",3,"Tuesday","No Match")

I can do the same thing with:

=TEXT(A2, "dddd")

So bad examples. Let's set that aside and think of some other option for how to use SWITCH. I think I would want to use it in a setting where I couldn't provide that response otherwise. My mind goes to my days of learning BASIC computer programming language when I was little and how you'd walk someone through a little choose your own adventure game.

Maybe I could set it up to ask someone a question and if they give me the right answer I give them one response. If they give me the wrong answer I give them another. Like this:

=SWITCH(A1,100,"Congratulations, that's correct.","Sorry, try again.")

That works. This is saying if the value in Cell A1 is 100 then put in this cell "Congratulations, that's correct." If it isn't, then put in this cell "Sorry, try again."

You could combine this with protecting the cells that use SWITCH so that users can't see what the answer is that's driving the response and basically use it to create self-directed quiz.

That's one option. What other use can we put this to?

What if we want to assign a salesperson to each account based upon letter of the alphabet? You could use SWITCH for that as well. I'm not going to write out the whole alphabet, but let's try a few letters. Here's the ugly, never want to do it again version which would require you to go into the function to swap things around each time someone left the company or joined it:

=SWITCH(LEFT(A1,1),"a","Jones","b","Smith","c","Carter","Harvey")

What that's saying is take the first letter of the value in Cell A1 and if that letter is an "a" assign it to Jones, if it's a "b" assign it to Smith, if it's a "c" assign it to Carter, and if it's any other letter assign it to Harvey.

We can transform that into a build-it-once, work-with-a-data-table-after-that version:

=SWITCH(LEFT(A1,1),G2,H2,G3,H3,G4,H4,H5)

Without context that second version is incomprehensible, but let's walk through it with reference to the version above where everything is in the formula itself.

All I've done in the second formula is put the values "a" and "Jones" in Cells G2 and H2, respectively. And then done the same thing for the remaining values, building a table that any user could see and interact with easily.

Either option would be a pain to build the first time out. But with the second one if I need to make edits I could make them to the data table not the formula.

Another thought. When I was trying to figure out why you'd use this I found someone mentioning that it's easier than using nested IF functions, which is probably true, but now that IFS exists, I don't think it's necessarily easier than IFS.

# Lookup Functions

Comparing the two, think of this one as not using the branching paths that IFS and nested IF functions do but more just a straight line list of alternatives.

Also, know that this function can take up to 126 values, although that would be quite a challenge to write the first time through.

Okay. On to another Excel function that you may or may not ever use but probably exists for a good reason, CHOOSE.

# The CHOOSE Function

**Notation:** CHOOSE(index_num, value1, [value2],…)

**Excel Definition:** Chooses a value or action to perform from a list of values, based on an index number

At its most basic, CHOOSE lets you pick a result from a list of values. So if the index_num is 2 then it picks the second value in your list. If it's 3 it picks the third value in the list. Which sounds pretty boring.

For me the power of CHOOSE lies in how it interacts with other functions, which is why I think the Excel help examples for this one vastly underplay what it can do. That's because the examples all use a fixed number for the index_num entry and the power in this function lies in having that index_num field be a calculation.

Let's walk through it and I'll show you what I mean.

The first input is an index_num that tells you which of the values to pick from a list. If it says 1, it picks the first value. If it says 2, it picks the second value. This number cannot be less than 1 nor can it be greater than the number of values you list in the function or else you'll get a #VALUE! error message.

You can, however, have a fraction for this value and Excel will truncate the value. So 2.33 becomes 2 and chooses the second listed option.

The rest of the function are your "values" or chosen outcomes. So:

$$=CHOOSE(2,23,43,54)$$

returns a result of 43. My index_num is 2 and the second value I provided was 43. If I change that 2 to a 5, I'll get an error. If it's less than 1 I get an error. If it's 3.45 that becomes 3 and my result is 54.

# Lookup Functions

So far, not something we really feel a need for, right?

What if instead of that 2, though, I used an IF function? Or a SWITCH function? Or the WEEKDAY function to give me a day of the week?

Here's a goofy little use of this:

=CHOOSE(WEEKDAY(F1),"Sunday is my fun day","Just another manic Monday","Tuesdays are boring","Wednesday, humpday")

This returns a saying for whatever the day of the week is for the date in Cell F1. Because the WEEKDAY function returns a number for the day of the week, we can then match that up with a saying for each day. (Who says uses of Excel always have to be serious?)

The only constraint there is that the index value you use in the first input needs to be a number from 1 to 254 and you need to have enough values after that to cover any index value your calculation comes up with. There's no last entry or default value that gets returned like with SWITCH or IFS.

We can also rewrite this one to replace the individual values with cell references:

=CHOOSE(WEEKDAY(F1),G2,G3,G4,G5)

In this case I've put the individual sayings in Cells G2 through G5. Much easier to work with after the fact.

So what's the difference between SWITCH and CHOOSE? They seem awfully similar, right?

SWITCH lets you specify specific results that return a chosen value. It's not limited to numeric results.

CHOOSE is a little less flexible. The index_num has to be a number. But it's easier to write if you're working with a numbered list and there are more values allowed.

One final note, your value inputs can be cell ranges as well. In the help text they use A1:A10, B1:B10, and C1:C10 as one set of values in a CHOOSE function formula. This is useful for when you nest CHOOSE within another function like SUM.

# The TRANSPOSE Function

**Notation:** TRANSPOSE(array)

**Excel Definition:** Converts a vertical range of cells to a horizontal range, or vice versa.

The TRANSPOSE function is one that you probably won't use very often, but it does come up. So let's walk through what TRANSPOSE does. It takes a series of entries that are in a column and displays them in a row instead or takes a series of entries that are in a row and displays them in a column.

You can do this with more than one row and/or column at a time. It will basically flip those entries so that what was in columns is now in rows and what was in rows is now in columns.

TRANSPOSE is a special kind of function that Excel introduced called an array formula. There are two key things to remember when working with array formulas.

First, you need to select a range of cells where your results will go *before* you start typing your formula in or it won't work.

Second, you need to use Ctrl + Shift + Enter when you're done entering your formula or it also won't work properly.

These two steps are what, for me, distinguish array formulas from other formulas. (That and the fact that the values they return appear in a range of cells instead of a single cell, of course because array formulas return multiple results.)

Let's walk through an example:

Let's say that in Cells A1 through A6 you have typed the numbers 1 through 6 and now you want those values across a row instead of in a column.

Go to where you want to put those values and highlight the entire range of cells where you want to put them. It needs to be the same size as the cells you're transposing, so in this case six cells.

# Lookup Functions

I'm going to highlight Cells E6 through J6 for this.
Keeping those cells highlighted, start typing your formula which is

$$=\text{TRANSPOSE(A1:A6)}$$

Finish with Ctrl + Shift + Enter.

If you've done it right, the numbers 1 through 6 will now also appear in Cells E6 through J6.

If you click on one of those cells, the formula in the formula bar should look like this for every one of those cells:

$$\{=\text{TRANSPOSE(A1:A6)}\}$$

Those squiggly brackets indicate an array formula.

Any change to the original cell range A1 through A6 will also change the value in the corresponding Cells E6 through J6. So if I replace 1 in Cell A1 with 10, that will also update Cell E6.

Now, the other option if you just want to change the orientation of your data is to copy and then use Paste Special-Transpose. To do this, select the cells you want to copy, click in the first cell where you want to paste that data (making sure enough cells are empty so you're not over-writing anything), and then right click, and under Paste Options choose the Transpose option. (The one with two little two-box grids with an arrow pointing between them in the bottom right corner of the clipboard image. For me, right now, that's the fourth image choice.)

You might wonder, if you can just copy and Paste Special-Transpose, why would you want to use this TRANSPOSE function instead? The key difference is that when you use the TRANSPOSE function your data it is still linked to the original source. That is not true with Paste Special-Transpose.

Also, you can pair TRANSPOSE with another array formula that would normally return results in a column to immediately return them in a row instead.

Basically, which option (function or pasting) is the better choice will depend on why you needed to do that. If you just wanted to transform a row of data into a column or vice versa, which is my usual reason for doing this, then Paste Special – Transpose is the easiest choice. If you're wanting to change the orientation of data that's output from an array formula or you want to copy data from one source and paste it to another in a different orientation while keeping the two sources linked, then the TRANSPOSE function will be the better option.

Just remember that when you use it it's an array formula so has to be set up and completed in a different manner than a normal function does.

# The INDEX Function

**Notation:** INDEX(array,row_num, [column_num]) or INDEX(reference, row_num, [column_num], [area_num])

**Excel Definition:** Returns a value or reference of the cell at the intersection of a particular row and column, in a given range.

The INDEX function can take two forms. It can be an array formula and return a range of values like we just saw TRANSPOSE do, or it can serve as a basic lookup formula and return a value from a specified column and row within a specified table.

When you open the help pane for this function it links to a video which gives a very nice overview of both ways of using the INDEX function, so I'd encourage you to watch that. But I'm going to walk through it here, too, so you don't have to if you don't want to.

At its most basic, the reference version

=INDEX(reference, row_num, [column_num], [area_num])

looks for a specific value in a specified position in a table. (To me this is much like how VLOOKUP and HLOOKUP work except it's not looking for a match to a value but a specific *location*.)

The first argument you provide in this version is the table you want to look in.

Let's say you have student grades for a series of tests and the data table is in Cells A2 through E7 with the actual data in Cells B3 through E7. Like so:

## Lookup Functions

|   | A | B | C | D | E |
|---|---|---|---|---|---|
| 1 |   | Semester 1 | | | |
| 2 |   | Test 1 | Test 2 | Test 3 | Test 4 |
| 3 | Student A | 82 | 87 | 94 | 92 |
| 4 | Student B | 88 | 81 | 84 | 83 |
| 5 | Student C | 65 | 68 | 64 | 63 |
| 6 | Student D | 98 | 98 | 98 | 99 |
| 7 | Student E | 86 | 88 | 84 | 83 |

If you want to extract from that table the grade on the third test for Student B, you could write either of the two following formulas using the INDEX function:

=INDEX(A2:E7,3,4)

or

=INDEX(B3:E7,2,3)

The difference between these two is the range of cells I told Excel to use for the reference data table. In the first one, Cells A2 through E7, I included the header row and column with the student names. In the second, Cells B3 through E7, I just included the results.

That's the first input into the INDEX function. The data range to use.

The second input is which row *in that range* to pull the data from. *This is not the actual row number in the worksheet.* This is which row *in your chosen range* to pull from.

So when I include the header row, Student B's data is in the third row of the data range. When I don't include the header row Student B's data is in the second row of the data range.

The third input is which column *in that range* to pull the data from. Same concept. Because in the first example I included the student names column, then to pull data for the third test we need to look at the fourth column in the data range. But in the second example where I only included the results, we pull from the third column.

There is a fourth input option that the INDEX function can use. It is very well demonstrated in that video that I referenced above, but I'll walk through it here as well.

The fourth input option works when you have more than one data table to look up values in. To use this option, the first input for the function has to include more than one data range. If you include more than one range in that first input then you can use the fourth input option for INDEX to tell Excel which of the multiple ranges you provided it should use.

(If you have not provided multiple ranges and specify a number for this fourth input you will get a #REF! error.)

Let's say that you teach the same group of students for two different semesters and so have test results for both of those semesters for the same students. Like this:

|   | A | B | C | D | E |
|---|---|---|---|---|---|
| 1 |   | Semester 1 | | | |
| 2 |   | Test 1 | Test 2 | Test 3 | Test 4 |
| 3 | Student A | 82 | 87 | 94 | 92 |
| 4 | Student B | 88 | 81 | 84 | 83 |
| 5 | Student C | 65 | 68 | 64 | 63 |
| 6 | Student D | 98 | 98 | 98 | 99 |
| 7 | Student E | 86 | 88 | 84 | 83 |
| 8 |   |   |   |   |   |
| 9 |   | Semester 2 | | | |
| 10 |   | Test 1 | Test 2 | Test 3 | Test 4 |
| 11 | Student A | 88 | 92 | 93 | 96 |
| 12 | Student B | 90 | 83 | 85 | 85 |
| 13 | Student C | 62 | 62 | 62 | 62 |
| 14 | Student D | 65 | 65 | 68 | 66 |
| 15 | Student E | 91 | 92 | 93 | 95 |

And now you want to pull the test score for the same student for the third test for each semester.

# Lookup Functions

First, let's pull the same data we pulled above, but with the INDEX formula set up to pull from either table, and specifying which table to use.

We can rewrite both formulas to include both table ranges and to pull from the first table like so:

$$=INDEX((A2:E7,A10:E15),3,4,1)$$

or

$$=INDEX((B3:E7,B11:E15),2,3,1)$$

Now we can modify both of those formulas to pull a value from the second table instead by changing the value of the last input in the function:

$$=INDEX((A2:E7,A10:E15),3,4,2)$$

or

$$=INDEX((B3:E7,B11:E15),2,3,2)$$

Of course, the way I would actually use this is not by manually going in and changing that final number each time. I would instead build a table that pulls in values from each semester. Like this:

|    | I | J | K | L |
|----|---|---|---|---|
| 8  |   | Test 3 Results | | |
| 9  |   |   |   |   |
| 10 |   |   | Semester | |
| 11 |   |   | 1 | 2 |
| 12 | Student A | 1 | 94 | 93 |
| 13 | Student B | 2 | 84 | 85 |

The formula I used here in Cell K12 is:

$$=INDEX(($A$2:$E$7,$A$10:$E$15),($J12+1),4,K$11)$$

That says that there are two tables of data to pull from with the given cell ranges and that the row to use is equal to the number in Column J plus 1. The column in each table to use is the fourth one, and that the table to pull from is the table number in Row 11.

I can then just copy that formula into all four cells and it will populate my table for me by looking in each of the semester grade tables for each student.

That to me has some potential value in extracting information from multiple tables to create a summary table.

The other potential value of the INDEX function is in its ability to pull an entire row or column of data out of a table. That is done by treating it as an array formula.

Remember from looking at the TRANSPOSE function that there are a few key things you need to do to treat a function as an array formula. (At least in Excel 2019.)

You have to select a range of cells not just one cell beforehand and then you have to use Ctrl + Shift + Enter after you've created the formula.

So let's go back to our two tables of data and let's extract all of the test scores for Student A using INDEX as an array formula, one row per semester, like this:

|    | I | J | K | L | M | N | O |
|----|---|---|---|---|---|---|---|
| 16 |   |   | Semester |   |   |   |   |
| 17 | Student A | 1 | 1 | 82 | 87 | 94 | 92 |
| 18 |   | 1 | 2 | 88 | 92 | 93 | 96 |

In Columns I, J, and K and Rows 17 and 18 I create a simple table with my semester number and my student row number so that I can use cell references to do this.

Once I've done that I highlight Cells L17 through O17 and then in L17 put the array formula:

=INDEX(($B$3:$E$7,$B$11:$E$15),J17,0,K17)

I finish by using Ctrl + Shift + Enter.

That's saying there are two tables and that I should pull the values from the table number listed in Cell K17. And I should then pull the row number listed in Cell J17. In this case, my table ranges are both just the data, so no need to adjust that value by adding one.

I just want the row of data, so for the column value I list 0.

# Lookup Functions

I then repeat that same process with Cells L18 through O18 to pull grades for the same student for the second semester.

(I will note here that you can't just copy and paste that second formula down like you would with a normal formula. It took a little fiddling to get it to copy down properly for me.)

In the same way that we extracted a row from a data table, you can also extract a column. Just make the row value 0 and provide a column value instead. Also, make sure that you highlight the number of cells needed for that specific column at the start.

And, to circle back to our TRANSPOSE function, if you wanted to return the column values as a row, you could pair the INDEX function with the TRANSPOSE function. So you could highlight five cells within a row and then use:

=TRANSPOSE(INDEX(($B$3:$E$7,$B$11:$E$15),0,3,1))

to pull the third column of data from the table of data contained in Cells B3 through E7 and put it in a row.

Keep in mind that these are still formulas, so if you change your source data you will change the values that you've pulled from the table. To lock any values into place use Paste Special – Values.

# The MATCH Function

**Notation:** MATCH(lookup_value, lookup_array, [match_type])

**Excel Definition:** Returns the relative position of an item in an array that matches a specified value in a specified order.

What MATCH is going to do for you is look in a range of cells, either a row or a column that you specify, and it is going to return for you the position of a specific value that you're looking for within that range.

You can also have it return the position of the closest value to what you're looking for rather than an exact match.

Note that this is a *position* (i.e. location) that you're getting back. It will tell you that that value you wanted is in the seventh row of the specified range. Or the third column of the specified range.

In and of itself, that's not going to do much for you. But where this becomes incredibly powerful is when you combine the MATCH function with other functions, like the INDEX function, to specify a row number or a column number.

So thinking back to what we did with INDEX, I can go back to that same table I had for student grades and I can use MATCH to look up the row number for each student and then combine that with the INDEX function to pull those student's grades on a specific test. Like so for Student A:

=INDEX(($A$2:$E$7),MATCH("Student A",$A$2:$A$7,0),4)

where I know that Column A in the table range has my student names in it.

The MATCH portion here is saying to find an exact match to "Student A" in Cells A2 through A7. That value is then used in the INDEX portion to say look in the cell range from Cells A2 through E7 and pull the value from the nth row where n is the value returned by the MATCH function and the 4th column.

I could go a step further and create a data table with all of my student names and then replace that "Student A" entry with a cell reference.

Pretty cool, huh? It requires a little twisting of your mind to get it to work, but this is incredibly powerful if you can do that.

A few things to know:

MATCH will look for a numeric value, a text value, or a logical value. It can also work with cell references.

There are three match types you can specify. Using a 0 means an exact match. Using a negative 1 means MATCH will find the smallest value that is greater than or equal to the specified lookup_value. Using a positive 1, so just 1, means MATCH will find the largest value that is less than or equal to the lookup_value.

If you use -1 or 1, you need to sort your data or it won't work properly; it will return a value of #N/A. For -1, sort your data in descending order. For 1, sort your data in ascending order.

Excel's default is to treat MATCH as if you've specified 1 as your match type, so be very very careful using MATCH since the default match type requires a specific sort order.

(I will note here that with all of these lookup functions I far prefer to use them for exact matches, because it's less likely I'll mess something up that way, but there are very good reasons to use them without wanting an exact match. You just have to be more careful.)

Keep in mind, too, that MATCH is not returning a row or column number. It is returning the *relative* row or column number *within your specified range of cells* which works perfectly in a scenario like the one above where we're using it in conjunction with the INDEX function, but would not work so well with say, macros.

Also, for text, MATCH does not distinguish between upper and lowercase letters.

If there is no match, MATCH will return a result of #N/A.

One of the reasons I included this function was because I saw an interesting use of the INDEX function when paired with the MATCH function that used MATCH and INDEX to pull in rank order of 34 different variables for a list of individuals. I'm not going to walk through it here because parsing it out would take about two pages of text, but just suffice it to say that you can get very complex results by using two simple functions like these together.

# Statistical Functions

Phew. Okay. That's the end of the Lookup Functions that we're going to cover. Now we get to blaze through a bunch of other functions that will be generally useful but are more focused on one specific calculation.

We're going to start with functions that Excel classifies as statistical functions, then we'll move on to the rest of the math functions, and then we'll wrap up with the text and date and time functions.

If you have a particular way in which you plan to use Excel that focuses more in one of these areas than another, this is the time to start skipping around.

This section will cover medians, modes, ranked values, linear forecasts, frequencies, and how to calculate the nth-largest or nth-smallest value in a range.

# The MEDIAN Function

**Notation:** MEDIAN(number1, [number2],…)

**Excel Definition:** Returns the median, or the number in the middle of the set of given numbers.

A calculation of the average of a range of values is very useful and very commonly used, but it can sometimes give very misleading results. That's where MEDIAN and MODE come in. They provide a better picture when your data is skewed in some way.

For example, writing income is highly skewed. (As is acting income.) There's someone out there making $100,000 a month and a lot of other someones out there making $10 a month. If you average those incomes you'll see an average of $10,000 a month, which looks really good. But the reality is that it's either be that one person making $100,000 a month or be everyone else making $10 a month. (It's not quite that bad. But it's close.)

An average won't show this, but the median will.

So if you don't know the nature of your data, it's always a good idea to take both the average and the median and compare them.

If the data is evenly distributed (spread out nicely) then they'll give you similar results. But if it's skewed, like in my example above, you'll have vastly different outcomes.

MEDIAN pretty works just like AVERAGE. All you do is use the function and give Excel the range of cells that contain you values. So

$$=MEDIAN(A1:A9)$$

will find the middle value out of the range of values in Cells A1 through A9.

It's that simple.

If you give Excel a range that has an even number of values, so there isn't just one middle value, Excel will average the two middle values and return their average. So

$$=MEDIAN(1,2,3,4)$$

will return 2.5 which is the average of the middle two values, 2 and 3.

(Be careful with this. Because =MEDIAN(1,100) would return a value of 50.5 which is very misleading since it's nowhere close to any actual potential value in the data. In general, it's a good idea to chart or visually inspect your data so you can see when situations like this exist.)

Median also works on logical values (TRUE, FALSE) that are typed directly into the argument. So =MEDIAN(TRUE,TRUE,FALSE) will return a value of 1 and =MEDIAN(FALSE,FALSE,TRUE) will return a value of 0. But if you reference a range with TRUEs and FALSEs in it you'll get a #NUM! error. I'm not sure how much good it does you that you can type it into the function directly, but that's the way it works.

(If you do ever have a set of TRUE/FALSE results, you can always convert them to ones and zeros using an IF function and then take the median of the ones and zeros.)

# The MODE.SNGL Function

**Notation:** MODE.SNGL(number1, [number2],…)

**Excel Definition:** Returns the most frequently occurring, or repetitive, value in an array or range of data.

As we discussed above, AVERAGE doesn't work well if your data has a high skew to it. So if most people score really low and there are just a few people who score really high then looking at an average is going to mislead you about how the average person will do. MEDIAN can sometimes be a better measure because it looks at the result in the exact middle.

But MEDIAN also has a flaw. And that's that it's not very good with data that has spikes that aren't near the middle of your data range. When that happens, sometimes it's best to look at the mode of your data. Excel 2019 has two options for doing this, MODE.SNGL and MODE.MULT.

MODE.SNGL is very simple to use.

$$=MODE.SNGL(A1:A10)$$

will calculate the mode for a range of values in Cells A1 through A10.

What MODE.SNGL basically does is count each value in your range and then returns the outcome with the highest count. But it has a flaw which is that if two values occur equally, it will only return the first of them because it can only return one value.

MODE.MULT which we'll talk about next can be used instead to find when there are multiple values that occur equally frequently.

# The MODE.MULT Function

**Notation:** MODE.MULT(number1, [number2],…)

**Excel Definition:** Returns a vertical array of the most frequently occurring, or repetitive, values in an array or range of data. For a horizontal array, use TRANSPOSE(MODE.MULT(number1,number2,…))

The MODE.MULT function allows Excel to return more than one value when it calculates the mode for a range of values. So if you have multi-modal data (meaning there are multiple bumps in your data), using MODE.MULT will return those multiple values where MODE.SNGL can't.

Now, there is a trick to using it because it is an array formula.

To use MODE.MULT you need a range of values that you're going to use for your mode calculation and a range of cells where you're going to put the result of that calculation.

Highlight the range of cells where you want your results to be displayed. You need to highlight enough cells to allow Excel to provide all possible values. (This is why plotting your data is a good idea. If you've plotted your data and seen that it has two equal-sized bumps in it, then you would know to highlight two cells. Otherwise you can guess and Excel will just return an #N/A value for the cells it didn't use.)

In the example at the end of this section, I highlighted Cells D5 through D8. Next, type in your formula. In the example below I typed:

$$=MODE.MULT(A1:A10)$$

to take the mode of the values in Cells A1 through A10.

*Then*, and this is crucial because it won't work otherwise, instead of typing Enter, you need to type Ctrl + Shift + Enter.

You'll know you've done it right, because when you click back into the cell the formula will have little brackets around it. Like this:

$$\{=MODE.MULT(A1:A10)\}$$

That exact same formula will appear in all of the cells you highlighted, not just the top one. And it will calculate the multiple modes in your data.

MODE.MULT also has a flaw. And that's that if you have one value that appears 99 times and another that appears 100 times, it will only return the value that appears 100 times even though they're almost identical results.

So let's put it all together to show AVERAGE, MEDIAN, MODE.SNGL, and MODE.MULT with a data set that is deliberately built to be multi-modal.

I've created a set of forty values that repeat the pattern 1, 3, 3, 3, 3, 30, 30, 30, 30, 500 four times. Here's a count table of those results and a graph of the values:

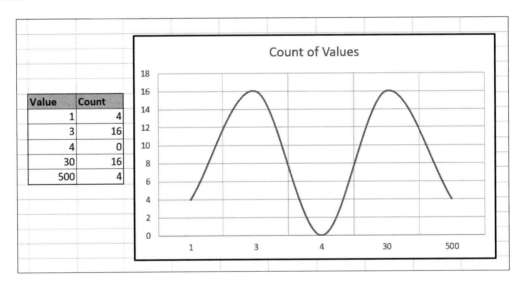

You can see from this graph that the v~alue of 3 and the value of 30 are the most commonly occurring values. They each occur 16 times in the data. The values of 1 and 500 each occur four times in the data. Those are the only possible outcomes: 1, 3, 30, 500.

Now, here are the calculations of the average, the median, the singular mode, and the multiple mode.

# Stastical Functions

| AVERAGE | 63.3 | =AVERAGE(A1:A40) |
|---|---|---|
| MEDIAN | 16.5 | =MEDIAN(A1:A40) |
| MODE.SNGL | 3 | =MODE.SNGL(A1:A40) |
| MODE.MULT | 3 | {=MODE.MULT(A1:A40)} |
| | 30 | {=MODE.MULT(A1:A40)} |
| | #N/A | {=MODE.MULT(A1:A40)} |
| | #N/A | {=MODE.MULT(A1:A40)} |

See the wide range of values you get?

Average is skewed higher than most outcomes because of the four 500 values in the data.

Median falls nowhere near an actual result that anyone will get because I have an even number of observations so it's showing the average between the two closest observations of 3 and 30. Despite that it does show a more realistic result than average in this case.

The single mode misses that 30 is just as likely an outcome as 3.

The multiple mode shows that the two equally frequent most common outcomes are 3 and 30 but it completely misses showing that 1 and 500 are possibilities as well. (Also, if either 3 or 30 were smaller by even one occurrence, it wouldn't show for MODE.MULT either. They have to be exactly equal in occurrence.)

So they all have their flaws.

That's why it's always a good idea to plot out your data to see what kind of patterns there are and to use multiple approaches to the data. (For example, this count table isn't the best for showing those outliers at 500 but a histogram would definitely show it.)

# The RANK.EQ Function

**Notation:** RANK.EQ(number, ref, [order])

**Excel Definition:** Returns the rank of a number in a list of numbers: its size relative to other values in the list; if more than one value has the same rank, the top rank of that set of values is returned.

In recent versions, Excel has taken what used to be the RANK function and designated it as RANK.EQ so that it can also have a RANK.AVG function. Both functions tell you the rank of a specified number within a range of values, but they each do it a little differently.

We'll start with RANK.EQ since that's the equivalent to the old RANK function.

The first input into the function is the number you're analyzing.

The next input is the overall range of numbers you want to compare it to. (The number can be pulled from the reference range and probably will be in most instances.)

The final input, order, tells Excel which way to rank things, from the highest number down or from the lowest number up. If you omit it, which you can, or use a zero (0), then Excel will rank based on descending order. If you use a one (1) or any other number other than zero, Excel will rank based on ascending order.

The sort order of the data in your reference range does not matter.

I placed the values 1 through 15 in Cells J1 through J15 and had Excel rank the 6 in that range using:

$$=RANK.EQ(6,J1:J15,0)$$

# Stastical Functions

This returned a value of 10 regardless of how the reference range was sorted. (Because if you start at 15 and count down, 6 will be the 10th value in the list.) Same with:

=RANK.EQ(6,J1:J15)

It also returned a value of 10. But

=RANK.EQ(6,J1:J15,1)

returned a value of 6 regardless of how the reference range was sorted because it was counting from 1 upward.

Be careful when using RANK.EQ if you have duplicates in your reference range. RANK.EQ assigns the same rank to duplicate values but then does not assign the next rank(s) to any value until it has skipped past the number of duplicates.

So if I have the numbers

1, 2, 2, 3, 4

and use an ascending rank order they would be ranked

1, 2, 2, 4, 5

respectively. If I used a descending rank order they would be ranked:

5, 3, 3, 2, 1

See how there are two ranks of 2 in that first example and two ranks of 3 in that second example? And how Excel skipped the rank of 3 in the first example and the rank of 4 in the second example?

If you have a tie like this the help text for the function gives a correction factor you can use.

Or you can use RANK.AVG which works just like RANK.EQ except it will average the ranks that would've been assigned to the tied values and return the average instead of the best rank.

So in the example above you'd have 1, 2.5, 2.5, 4, 5 or 5, 3.5, 3.5, 2, 1 as your result depending on the sort order.

127

## The SMALL Function

**Notation:** SMALL(array, k)

**Excel Definition:** Returns the k-th smallest value in a data set. For example, the fifth smallest number.

The SMALL function will look at a range of values and return the kth smallest value in the range where k is the number you specify.

It's pretty straight-forward. The first input is the cell range you want to use and the second input is a number representing the position in the range you're interested in.

If you want the smallest value in Column A (and didn't want to use MIN for some reason), you could use

=SMALL(A:A,1)

to return it. But more likely you're going to want something like the 10th smallest value which would be:

=SMALL(A:A,10)

Your array can also cover more than one row or column. So:

=SMALL(A1:B5,3)

would return the 3rd smallest value in Cells A1 through B5.

## Stastical Functions

Technically, you could also use SMALL to return the *largest* value in an array if you knew the number of values in the array. Depending on your data this could be done with the COUNT function like so:

=SMALL(A1:B5,COUNT(A1:B5))

But, better yet, there's the LARGE function which does exactly what the SMALL function does but for the k-th largest value in a data set.

With either LARGE or SMALL, if you use a value for k that is larger than the count of the numeric values in the range, you will get a #NUM! error message as your result. So if I had text in one of the cells above and used COUNTA instead of COUNT that wouldn't have worked.

# The FORECAST.LINEAR Function

**Notation:** FORECAST.LINEAR(x, known_ys, known_xs)

**Excel Definition:** Calculates, or predicts, a future value along a linear trend by using existing values.

Excel provides a couple of interesting functions that are designed to forecast future values based on existing data. We're just going to cover the basic linear forecast function, FORECAST.LINEAR, here but you can also use an exponential smoothing forecast option, FORECAST.ETS for when your data isn't linear and/or has seasonality to it.

The FORECAST.LINEAR function replaced the old FORECAST function.

Now, one thing to note right up front is that this function assumes a linear trend in your data. So the plotting example I used in *Excel 2019 Intermediate* for scatter plots that involved calculating time to hit the ground when an object is dropped from different heights would not work with FORECAST.LINEAR since that's not a linear relationship.

Which means you should definitely plot your data before you apply this forecast function to it to see if it's following a general linear trend.

The way FORECAST.LINEAR works is you give Excel a table of known x and y combinations and Excel then uses those data points to create the best linear fit through the points.

You then tell Excel your x value that you want to predict y for.

Your x values must be numbers otherwise you will get a #VALUE! error.

You also must provide an equal number of x's and y's that have values. If they don't match up or one is empty you will get a #N/A error message.

If there is no variance in your x values you will get a #DIV/0! error message.

## Stastical Functions

If you want to know the formula Excel uses to do this calculation, it's in the help documentation for the function.

Now let's walk through an example. Here's a data table where I've put number of customers in the store and number of sales in a data table. I've built this data so that for every two customers who walk through the door, the store gets a sale.

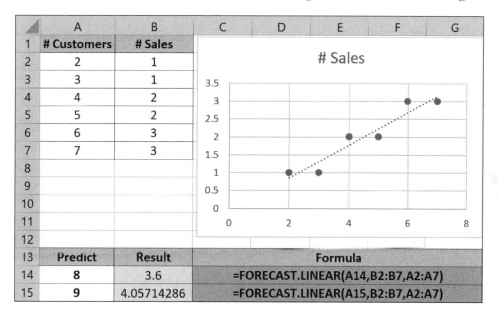

I've also plotted the results so that you can see it is a generally linear progression, although not perfectly linear and I've added a linear trendline to that plot to show the line that Excel is calculating behind the scenes to make its predictions with this function.

Below the table I have used FORECAST.LINEAR to predict the number of sales when there are 8 customers and 9 customers in the store. (Because this is artificial data we know the answer for both should be 4.)

The first formula I used was:

=FORECAST.LINEAR(A14,B2:B7,A2:A7)

where the value 8 was in Cell A14.

As you can see, the predictions that Excel came up with for 8 and 9 customers were 3.6 and 4.06 because it's trying to draw the best line it can through the data and that best line falls between the actual data points.

Now, one thing to point out here, because it tripped me up the first time I used the function, is that you list all of your *y values* before you list all of your x values. This was backwards to me since every point coordinate I ever remember seeing was written x, y.

Also, if you ever try to use FORECAST.LINEAR for time series data (and I have with FORECAST) understand that your x values are numbers to Excel not dates so 0 is a valid x value. Meaning if you try to predict a prior value from your data range you need to account for 0 representing one of your observations. If 1 is January 2019, then 0 is December 2018.

(This is why it's always good to gut check the results you get to see if they make sense given the data.)

One final note. Even though in the example above I had the data points sorted by x-value, you don't need to do that. Your data can be out of order and Excel will still be able to work with it effectively when using FORECAST.LINEAR.

If you have data where the order matters (like monthly sales data, for example), especially if the data is not linear then considering using FORECAST.ETS instead.

# The FREQUENCY Function

**Notation:** FREQUENCY(data_array, bins_array)

**Excel Definition:** Calculates how often values occur within a range of values and then returns a vertical array of numbers having one more element than Bins_array.

Earlier we talked about how to use functions to calculate the average, median, and mode, and as part of doing so I pointed out that one of the drawbacks of even MODE.MULT is that it only cares about the most frequently occurring value or values. So if you have a value that appears 29 times and one that appears 28 times, MODE.MULT will only return the value that appears 29 times.

One way to get around this is by building a frequency table which we're going to do using the FREQUENCY function.

The first input into the FREQUENCY function is your data.

We're going to work with a set of values where we have the number 1 one time, the number 3 four times, the number 30 three times, and the number 500 twice. (See below.)

So 3 is the most frequently occurring value but 30 comes in close behind.

(If I were to use MODE.MULT on this data range I would get the result of 3 back, but nothing else. I want more detail than that and that's where FREQUENCY comes in.)

The second input into the function is what's called the bins array. This is how we tell Excel to bucket the results. If we want exact counts of every value in our data range then we can remove duplicates from our initial data set and use those as our bins. That will give a unique count for every value in the table.

If we're okay having values from 0 to 25 grouped together and then up to 50 grouped together, etc. we could tell Excel our bins are 25, 50, and so on.

Below I've taken both approaches. My first table has 1, 3, 30, and 500 as my bins. My second table has 25, 50, 500, and then a blank cell as my bins to cover anything over 500.

FREQUENCY is an array function so you have to highlight all of the cells where you want your results to be displayed before you type the function. You can then type in the function and use Shift + Ctrl + Enter to finish.

This is what we get for both approaches:

| | A | B | C | D | E F G |
|---|---|---|---|---|---|
| 1 | Values | | Bins | Count | Formula |
| 2 | 1 | | 1 | 1 | =FREQUENCY(A2:A11,C2:C5) |
| 3 | 3 | | 3 | 4 | =FREQUENCY(A2:A11,C2:C5) |
| 4 | 3 | | 30 | 3 | =FREQUENCY(A2:A11,C2:C5) |
| 5 | 3 | | 500 | 2 | =FREQUENCY(A2:A11,C2:C5) |
| 6 | 3 | | | | |
| 7 | 30 | | Bins | Count | Formula |
| 8 | 30 | | 25 | 5 | =FREQUENCY(A2:A11,C8:C11) |
| 9 | 30 | | 50 | 3 | =FREQUENCY(A2:A11,C8:C11) |
| 10 | 500 | | 500 | 2 | =FREQUENCY(A2:A11,C8:C11) |
| 11 | 500 | | | 0 | =FREQUENCY(A2:A11,C8:C11) |

The formula in the first example where the bins are 1, 3, 30, and 500 is

$$=FREQUENCY(A2:A11,C2:C5)$$

And because this is an array formula that is the formula for all of the rows of the table, not just the first one.

The formula in the second example where the bins are 25, 50, 500, and blank is:

$$=FREQUENCY(A2:A11,C8:C11)$$

Both formulas are doing the exact same thing. They are counting the number of values that are less than or equal to the first value in each table and then from there up to the second value in the table and so on. The reason the results are different is because of the bins we chose.

So you can use FREQUENCY for precise counts of each value, like we did in the first example, or for counts across a range of values, like in the second example. You just have to structure your bins correctly.

And remember to highlight enough cells when inputting the function to cover the less than and more than portions of the range. In the second example, I had four bin inputs but needed to highlight five cells when I built my table to account for any possible values over 500.

Also, FREQUENCY will ignore blank cells and text, so if you want the FREQUENCY of text values, you can't use it. It only works with numbers.

And remember, this is an array function, so always highlight all of your cells where you want your answers before you input your function and use Shift + Ctrl + Enter when you're done or you won't get the right results.

# More Math Functions

Okay. Now on to more functions that Excel categorizes as Math & Trig functions. This section covers functions that round values, take the sum product, provide the square root, etc. I'm pretty sure none of the functions I'm covering here would actually be classified as trig functions but they do exist. So if you need sine and cosine, etc. this is the category they'd fall under in the function library.

# The SUMPRODUCT Function

**Notation:** SUMPRODUCT(array1, [array2], [array3],…)

**Excel Definition:** Returns the sum of the products of corresponding ranges or arrays.

You use SUMPRODUCT when you have a range of cells that need the values in each position in the range to be multiplied times one another (like number of units and price to get total cost for a specific transaction) and then the results summed (to get total cost, for example).

SUMPRODUCT is incredibly useful when you need it. You could get the same result using a combination of SUM and PRODUCT, but why do that when one little function will do it for you? (I'm not going to cover PRODUCT separately here, but it basically takes whatever values you give it and multiplies them times one another.)

Now, that definition and the use of "array" in the Excel notation for the function probably seem a little intimidating. Don't worry, they're not.

Let's walk through an example with units and price:

|   | A | B | C | D |
|---|---|---|---|---|
| 1 | Product | Units | Price | Total |
| 2 | Widgets | 4 | $ 2.25 | $ 9.00 |
| 3 | Whatsits | 5 | $ 3.50 | $ 17.50 |
| 4 | Whatchamacallits | 3 | $ 6.00 | $ 18.00 |
| 5 | Whatnots | 2 | $ 4.00 | $ 8.00 |
| 6 |   |   |   | $ 52.50 |

## More Math Functions

What we have here is a list of products bought by a customer. We have product name, number of units bought, and price paid per unit.

In Column D I've calculated the total to the customer the old-fashioned way. I've taken Units times Price for each row and then totaled those values to get the total for the customer in Cell D6.

Now let's use SUMPRODUCT for that same calculation:

| 8 | Calculated Result | Formula |
|---|---|---|
| 9 | $ 52.50 | =SUMPRODUCT(B2:B5,C2:C5) |

In Cell A9 I've made that same calculation but with the SUMPRODUCT function:

=SUMPRODUCT(B2:B5,C2:C5)

That says, take the values in Cells B2 through B5 and the values in Cells C2 through C5 and then multiply B2 times C2, B3 times C3, etc. and add together the results to return a total.

A few things to be aware of. The ranges you input into the function need to be the same size for this to work. If they aren't you will get a #VALUE! result instead.

Also, be sure that the ranges you choose have numbers in them and not text. Excel will treat non-numeric values as zeros and any number times zero is…zero.

And, while the example I used above had values in two columns you are not limited to just two columns of values. (Just be sure the cells you select should be multiplied by one another and then added. So I could've had another column in there for sales tax, for example.)

You can also use SUMPRODUCT with values that are in rows instead or columns or in a combination of rows and columns. The key is that the ranges you specify have to be the same dimension, so the same number of columns and rows. (And obviously it needs to make sense.)

Okay, now let's talk about absolute value.

# The ABS Function

**Notation:** ABS(number)

**Excel Definition:** Returns the absolute value of a number, a number without its sign.

The ABS function essentially converts any number you have into a positive number. I could see this being useful if you are calculating, say, a ratio of two numbers and it doesn't matter whether one or both of those numbers is negative, you just want the ratio as a positive number.

So, for example, if I had -6 in Cell A1 and 2 in Cell A2 and wanted the ratio of those two numbers as a positive value, I could use:

$$=ABS(A1/A2)$$

or

$$=ABS(A1)/A2$$

Either way my result would be 3. If I had just divided those two numbers without using ABS the result would have been -3.

That's pretty much it.

(Interestingly enough, if you have numbers stored as text a function like SUM or PRODUCT will not work on them, but ABS still does.)

# The POWER Function

**Notation:** POWER(number, power)

**Excel Definition:** Returns the result of a number raised to a power.

POWER is a function that will let you raise any number to any power. But as a reminder first, you don't need a function to do powers. You can just use the little caret symbol (^) and input your power that way. So

$$=3\wedge 2$$

returns the value of three squared which is 9.
And

$$=9\wedge.5$$

returns the value for the square root of 9 which is 3.

As you can see with these examples, you use whole numbers to take a number to a power and decimals to take the root of a number.

You can also use negative powers to indicate that the number is part of the denominator. (So =3^-2 is the same as 1 divided by three squared or 1/9.)

The caret works with cell references, too. So

$$=A1\wedge A2$$

would take the value in Cell A1 and raise it to the power of the value in Cell A2.

But you can also use the POWER function for this, so let's cover it.

It's very simple. The first value is the number you want to take to a power, the second number is the power you want to use.

So three squared would be

$$=POWER(3,2)$$

And the square root of 9

$$=POWER(9,.5)$$

The power can also be a negative number which, as mentioned above, puts the value in the denominator. So

$$=POWER(3,-2)$$

is the same as 1 divided by 3 squared.

You can also put a complex calculation or a cell reference in for either of the inputs:

$$=POWER(A1,A2)$$

for example.

Just like you learned in math class, if the power is 0 then the result is 1.

If you are specifically taking the square root of a value, you can use the SQRT function instead. And the SQRTPI function will take the square root of the product of a number and pi.

Also, if you're working with natural logarithms, the EXP function will return the value of *e* raised to a given power. This means that you can also use =EXP(1) to derive the value of *e* if you need it.

# The PI Function

**Notation:** PI( )

**Excel Definition:** Returns the value of Pi, 3.14159265358979, accurate to 15 digits.

The PI function is another function that can make life simpler when working with complex formulas. If you need to do a calculation that involves the number pi, 3.14 etc. etc., using the PI function will return that value for you accurate up to the 15th digit.

So, for example, the area of a circle can be calculated using pi times the square of the radius. Let's assume radius is in Cell A1.

I could write

$$=PI(\ )*(A1\wedge 2)$$

to make that calculation.

Note that when I use the function PI I need to include those opening and closing parens to let Excel know that's what I'm doing. You don't put anything in them, though.

If you just want the value of pi in a cell type

$$=PI(\ )$$

in that cell and hit enter.

(Also, you don't need that space in between the parens. It will work with or without it.)

# The LOG Function

**Notation:** LOG(number, [base])

**Excel Definition:** Returns the logarithm of a number to the base you specify.

The LOG function does just what it says, it returns the logarithm of a number to the specified base. The default is to assume that you're working with base 10. So if you don't provide a second value in the function and just write

$$=\text{LOG}(10)$$

it will assume that the base you meant it to use is base 10. That means the answer you'll get is 1. Because 10 to the what power gives you 10? 1

That's why

$$=\text{LOG}(1000)$$

is 3. Because 10 to what power gives you 1000? 3

If you want to work with a different base than 10, say 2, you just put that into the function as your second argument. So

$$=\text{LOG}(32,2)$$

is asking what power you have to take 2 to to get 32. (That's a mouthful of 2's isn't it?) Answer, 5.

For natural logs you can use the EXP function with the LOG function. Like so:

# More Math Functions

$$=LOG(86,EXP(1))$$

This will return for you the power to which you have to take *e* to get a value of 86, which is approximately 4.45.

Excel also has the LN function which is built to work with natural logs where

$$=LOG(86,EXP(1))$$

and

$$=LN(86)$$

will return the same result.

There is also the LOG10 function for base 10 where

$$=LOG10(100)$$

and

$$=LOG(100)$$

will return the same result.

# The FACT Function

**Notation:** FACT(number)

**Excel Definition:** Returns the factorial of a number, equal to 1*2*3*…*Number.

The FACT function returns the factorial of a number which is used in calculating permutations. So

$$=FACT(3)$$

will give you a value of 6 which is equal to 3 times 2 times 1. And

$$=FACT(4)$$

will give you a value of 24 which is equal to 4 times 3 times 2 times 1.

If you try to use a number that is not a whole number with the FACT function Excel will truncate it to a whole number. So

$$=FACT(4.567)$$

returns the same value as =FACT(4)

(Note that's a truncation not rounding. 4.567 became a 4 not a 5.)

Also, keep in mind that you can't have a factorial of a negative number and that the factorial of zero is returned as a value of 1 since that's standard practice when working with factorials.

## The COMBIN Function

**Notation:** COMBIN(number, number_chosen)

**Excel Definition:** Returns the number of combinations for a given number of items.

You can use factorials to calculate the number of combinations in a given population, but Excel has provided two functions that will do this for you.

The COMBIN function calculates the number of combinations given a population size and sample size without repetition. So with the numbers 1, 2, and 3 you can have 12 as a possible combination but not 11.

The inputs to the COMBIN function are your population size and your sample size. So

$$=COMBIN(3,2)$$

is asking how many combinations of 1, 2, and 3 you can have if you choose two at a time and don't repeat. The answer is 3 for 12 or 21, 23 or 32, and 13 or 31.

If you do want to allow for repetition then the function to use is COMBINA. It has the same inputs, population size and sample size, but

$$=COMBINA(3,2)$$

returns a value of 6 because with repetitions you can also have 11, 22, and 33 as possible combinations.

# Text Functions

Excel has a number of text functions that can come in handy. Functions that let you transform text to upper or lower case, select just a portion of an entry, and transform certain values to their text equivalent. You can also use text functions to search for a specific result which is useful when combined with other functions as well as if you ever venture into using macros.

Let's cover some of those now.

# The UPPER Function

**Notation:** UPPER(text)

**Excel Definition:** Converts a text string to all uppercase letters.

The UPPER function has a very simple purpose, and that is to take a text entry and convert it to all uppercase letters.

So, for example,

$$=UPPER("test")$$

will return TEST. Or, if you had the word "test" in Cell B2 and you wrote

$$=UPPER(B2)$$

it would also return the value TEST.

You cannot reference more than once cell at a time using UPPER. However, you can combine the UPPER function with other functions to return a result that is in upper case letters.

For example,

$$=UPPER(TEXTJOIN(" ",1,A1:A2))$$

would return the text in Cells A1 and A2 with a space between them and all in upper case letters.

If you want all lower case letters, you can use the LOWER function. And to have a text string where the first letter of each word is capitalized and the rest is in lower case, use PROPER.

# The LEFT Function

**Notation:** LEFT(text, [num_chars])

**Excel Definition:** Returns the specified number of characters from the start of a text string.

The LEFT function allows you to extract the left-most portion of a text string.

This can be a useful function if you only want a portion of a standardized entry. For example, for a driver's license number that starts with a two-digit year, then a dash, then the license number, to extract the year portion, you could use

$$=LEFT(B2,2)$$

assuming the value was in Cell B2. That would give you just the year portion of that license number.

Note that the definition says it works on a text string, but I was able to also get it to work on a number. So

$$=LEFT(1234,2)$$

returns 12.

You can accomplish the same thing with Text to Columns using Fixed Width, but LEFT is a better option when all you want is that one portion of the entry and you don't need the rest of it.

Other identifiers that might be similarly structured include customer identification numbers and social security numbers.

The number of characters specified must be greater than or equal to zero.

If the number of characters you specify is greater than the length of the text entry, Excel will return the full text entry.

If you omit the number of characters, Excel will extract the left-most character only. So

$$=\text{LEFT}(\text{``test''})$$

will return a result of t.

The RIGHT function works exactly like the LEFT function but it returns the specified number of characters from the end (or right-hand side) of the text string.

For languages such as Chinese, Japanese, and Korean you may need to use LEFTB or RIGHTB functions instead and specify the number of bytes rather than the number of characters. This also applies for the next function we're going to cover, the MID function, where you'd use MIDB.

# The MID Function

**Notation:** MID(text, start_num, num_chars)

**Excel Definition:** Returns the characters from the middle of a text string, given a starting position and length.

The MID function works much like the LEFT and RIGHT functions except it extracts characters from the middle of an entry. Because of this, it requires one more input, the start number. So you have to tell Excel which character in your string should be the first character pulled and then how many characters you want after that.

For example, for a social security number if you want the middle two digits of the value stored in Cell B2 you would use

$$=MID(B2,5,2)$$

assuming the number was written as XXX-XX-XXXX.

Be sure to count each space, dash, etc. in your determination of the start number.

If your start number is greater than the number of characters in your referenced text, Excel will return an empty text entry.

If you ask for more characters to be returned than exist, Excel will return what there is. So

$$=MID("advice",3,7)$$

will returned "vice" even though that's only four characters.

Your start number must be equal to or greater than 1. Your number of characters must be equal to or greater than zero.

# The TEXT Function

**Notation:** TEXT(value, format_text)

**Excel Definition:** Converts a value to text in a specific number format.

The TEXT function is an interesting one, because it really has two completely different uses, one for formatting and one for extracting a name for day of the week or month from a date.

I'm going to cover the usage here that interests me and that's the second one, it's ability to extract the name for the day of the week or the month from a date.

(If you're interested in its other use, check out the help section which goes into incredible detail on all the possibilities. Just be careful because it's possible to format your entries in ways that do not make sense at all using TEXT.)

Okay.

So using TEXT you can take a date, like 4/4/2018, and you can have Excel return for you the name of the day of the week or the month associated with that date. So Wednesday or April in this case.

I find that very useful, and recently used it when I was trying to create a table with day of the week across the top but only had dates to work with.

To extract the name of the day of the week, use

$$=\text{TEXT}(A1,\text{"dddd"})$$

or

$$=\text{TEXT}(A1,\text{"ddd"})$$

Assuming the date is in Cell A1 that will give you the full name for the day of the week (Tuesday) in the first example or the abbreviated day of the week (Tue) in the second example.

To extract the name of the month, use

$$=\text{TEXT(A1,"mmmm")}$$

or

$$=\text{TEXT(A1,"mmm")}$$

That will give you the full month (January) in the first example or the abbreviated month (Jan) in the second example.

# The LEN Function

**Notation:** LEN(text)

**Excel Definition:** Returns the number of characters in a text string.

The LEN function returns a numeric value representing the number of characters in a text string. (Note that for some languages like Japanese, Chinese, or Korean that you may instead need the LENB function which returns the number of bytes in a text string.)

You can use LEN with text directly in the function or with a cell reference.

The count includes spaces as well as actual characters. So

$$=\text{LEN}(\text{"One day"})$$

will return a value of 7 for the o-n-e-space-d-a-y in "one day".

I could also type my text in Cell A1 and then use

$$=\text{LEN}(A1)$$

to get the same result.

If there is a formula in a cell that is referenced by LEN, it will count the number of characters in the result of the formula not the formula itself. (Which is good.)

If a cell is empty or has a "" value, LEN will return a value of zero.

You might be asking yourself when you would use this function.

One possibility is when you want to remove standardized text from a longer text string.

# Text Functions

You could pair LEN with a function like LEFT, RIGHT, or MID to extract the remainder of your text.

For example, let's say I have the following entries:

12,500 units

5,122 units

312 units

And I want just the numbers without the space or "units" included. Assuming that first value is in Cell A1, I could use

=LEFT(A1,LEN(A1)-LEN(" units"))

and then copy that formula down the next two rows to extract just the numbers from those entries.

This works because all of the entries have the same text at the end, " units" that I want to remove.

Because the number of units isn't the same between each one, that is probably the only way to trim that off using a function. (You could also use the Text to Columns option on the Data tab as an alternative way to split the number from the units, but it would then require deleting the column of data you don't want so would require an additional step.)

Another function you could use for tasks similar to LEN is SEARCH. SEARCH will tell you the number of the character in a text string at which the text you care about first appears, moving from left to right.

# The EXACT Function

**Notation:** EXACT(text1, text2)

**Excel Definition:** Checks whether two text strings are exactly the same, and returns TRUE or FALSE. EXACT is case-sensitive.

The EXACT function compares two text strings to see if they're exactly the same or not. I've used a simple IF function to do the same thing before, but this is easier to write.

What I've needed it for in the past was to see if two sets of data that I was trying to compare had entries in the same order. I used to use some advertising reports where the entity providing me with data would insert new ads in the midst of the old data and if I tried to compare an old report to a new report I'd end up comparing results for Ad 10 with results for Ad 35.

To fix that I would sort the report and then check that I had the ads lined up properly using an IF function that looked something like this:

=IF(B2=P2,"","ERROR")

That's saying, do the text values in Cell B2 and Cell P2 match? If so, good. If not, tell me there's an error.

But I could have used the EXACT function instead and written:

=EXACT(B2,P2)

**Text Functions**

If the two values match it returns a value of TRUE. If they don't it returns a value of FALSE.

The function is case-sensitive, but will ignore any differences in formatting.

Once you have your TRUE and FALSE values you can then filter for the ones that have an issue or use search or just scan the list.

# Date & Time Functions

Alright. On to the date and time functions. If you're not going to use them much you can probably skip what I'm about to discuss, but since it's tripped me up a few times when I needed to work with dates I wanted to be sure to cover some quirks to how dates are treated in Excel.

Excel actually encodes each date as a number starting with the number 1 for the date January 1, 1900 and then moving forward one number at a time for each subsequent date. You can test this by typing the number 1 into a cell and then formatting that cell as a date. As soon as you format that cell as a date you will see January 1, 1900 in that cell. This is important for a few reasons.

First, it means that Excel does not do well with dates prior to 1900. I learned this the hard way on a work project that had dates back to the 1700s when I found that Excel had converted those 1700s and 1800s dates to 1900s dates after they were imported from a SQL database into Excel. So it's something to keep an eye on if you're working with older dates.

Second, because Excel encodes dates as numbers this means that simple addition and subtraction works on dates in Excel. If you want a date fifteen days in the future, you just add 15 to the current date. So say that date is stored in Cell A1, then you'd write =A1+15 and Excel would return a date for you that is 15 days past the date in Cell A1. If you wanted a date that was 14 days *prior* to that date then you would write =A1-14.

As long as the dates remain in the range of January 1, 1900 to December 31, 9999 you're fine.

This also means that Excel converts hours, minutes, and seconds into decimals. So .5 is the equivalent of 12 hours, .041667 is a single hour, .000694 is a minute, and .00001157 is one second.

Third, the fact that dates are encoded as numbers means that any date functions that mention a serial_number as the input are actually telling you to input the date that you want to use.

Now, to put a wrinkle in this, if someone is using a Mac instead of a PC and Excel 2008 for Mac or earlier what I said above about the date range covered by Excel is not accurate. In that case Excel actually started with the date January 2, 1904 and moved forward from there. This was fixed in Excel for Mac 2011. The dates should convert automatically when moving between the two, but be careful if you're working with someone who has a Mac version of Excel.

One option to avoid these kinds of issues with dates that are out of range or dates that appear as one date in one version and another date in another version is to store your dates as text instead of dates unless you need them to be dates for calculation purposes.

(This may also be a good time to point out that Excel is not necessarily the ideal option for handling large amounts of complex data. It's great for basic usage and calculations but when you really get into data it's probably time to use something else. For example, I've worked with R, Stata, and SQL databases when dealing with large amounts of data.)

Also…

Best practice when dealing with dates in Excel is to enter the four-digit year. So if I want January 1, 2019 it is best to enter that date as 1/1/2019 so that Excel knows exactly what date I want. If you leave off the first two numbers of the year, so use 1/1/19 instead, Excel will convert that to a four-digit year using the following logic:

As of now, numbers 00 through 29 are interpreted as the years 2000 through 2029. Numbers 30 through 99 are interpreted as the years 1930 through 1999.

To avoid this being an issue as we approach 2029, I'd recommend that you always try to enter four digits for every year so that this is never an issue for you.

(And if you want to read up on all of this more it's under the Excel help topic "change the date system, format, or two-digit year interpretation.")

Good times.

Okay, then. Now that we have a basic understanding of how dates are handled by Excel, let's look at some date-related functions.

# The DATE Function

**Notation:** DATE(year, month, day)

**Excel Definition:** Returns the number that represents the date in Microsoft Excel date-time code.

I don't use the DATE function regularly but we need to discuss it first because in the help text for most of the date and time functions Excel has a caution that dates used in each function should be created using the DATE function or as results of other formulas or functions. The implication is that if you don't do this your results may not be fully accurate.

In general, I don't think you'll have an issue using a date you've typed in. For example,

$$1/1/11$$

$$1\text{-}1\text{-}11$$

$$1/1/2011$$

$$1\text{-}1\text{-}2011$$

January 1, 2011

all work as long as you keep in mind what we discussed above about how Excel handle dates.

But if it's vitally important that your date calculations be accurate then maybe use the DATE function.

So how does it work?

For the most basic usage, you input a value for year, month, and day and Excel turns it into a numeric value representing a date. For example:

$$=DATE(1900,1,1)$$

will return a value that displays as 1/1/1900 and is automatically formatted as a date.

There are, however some definite quirks with this function. The worst one is that if you input a year value between 0 and 1899, Excel will *add* that value to 1900 to calculate your year.

It's the most ridiculous thing I've ever seen, but that's how it works. (An error message would've been better in my opinion.)

So

$$=DATE(1880,1,1)$$

which you would hope returns a date of January 1, 1880 will actually return a date of 1/1/3780.

A reminder that if you're going to work with dates in Excel you must drill into your head that they only work between the years of 1900 and 9999. Also, a good reason to always have your dates display with a four-digit year so you can see when this happens, because 1/1/80 looks like it could be 1/1/1880 like you intended even though it's actually 1/1/3780.

With the DATE function if you put in a year that's less than 0 or past 9999 you do get an error message, the #NUM! error.

DATE can do more than just create a date from your inputs. It can also take an existing date and by adding values to year, month, and day create a new date. For this reason, you can enter any value you want for month and for day.

If the value for month is greater than 12, Excel will add that number of months to the first month in the year specified. So

$$=DATE(1900,14,1)$$

returns a date of February 1, 1901, which is two months into the next year. And

$$=DATE(1900,38,1)$$

## Date & Time Functions

returns a date of February 1, 1903, which is two months into the year three years from 1900.

If you enter a negative value for month, Excel will subtract "the magnitude of that number of months, plus 1, from the first month in the year specified."

I find that wording horrible.

What you have to keep in mind is that when you go backwards, Excel includes the value of zero as a legitimate value. So if I use

$$=DATE(1905,-2,1)$$

Excel returns a date of October 1, 1904 which is *three* months prior to January. To get a date of December 1, 1904, I have to use

$$=DATE(1905,0,1)$$

The same thing happens with days of the month. If you're going negative you have to adjust by 1 because of the fact that Excel will take a value of 0 as the value for one day prior and then work from there.

I'd be very careful using DATE to go backward for this very reason. It's far too easy to mess up if you're not paying attention, so check, double-check, triple-check your results.

Now let's walk through the more complex usage for DATE and the reason all the craziness exists.

The DATE function can be used in conjunction with other functions or basic math to create new dates.

So, for example, you can create a date five years from now by taking a date that's in Cell A1 and combining that with the DATE function as well as the YEAR, MONTH, and DAY functions to extract the values for year, month, and date, respectively. This is more precise than adding 365 times 5 days to that date because it won't be impacted by something like leap year.

What does that look like?

Assuming your date is stored in Cell A1 and you want a date five years from that date, you would write:

$$=DATE(YEAR(A1)+5,MONTH(A1),DAY(A1))$$

That's saying, take the year from the date in Cell A1 and add 5 to it. Then take the month from the date in Cell A1 and the day from the date in Cell A1, and build a date with those values.

If Cell A1 was January 1, 2015 you would now have a date of January 1, 2020.

If we had instead used five times 365 days and added that to the date in Cell A1, so =A1+1825, we would end up with a date in 2019, specifically December 31, 2019, because of the existence of a leap year in that date range.

So use DATE if you want to create a new date x number of years or months in the future. Use math if you want to create a date x number of days in the future.

Also, just to note that if I had wanted to use the date directly in the formula instead of a cell reference, I would need to use quotation marks to do so, like this:

$$="1/1/2015"+(365*5)$$

(I've sort of cheated here by using a date that has the same month and day because I suspect the required format for that date entry will vary across country depending on whether you're in a month/day country or a day/month country.)

Alright, now that we used it in an example let's actually walk through the YEAR function.

# The YEAR Function

**Notation:** YEAR(serial_number)

**Excel Definition:** Returns the year of a date, an integer in the range 1900-9999.

The YEAR function extracts the four-digit year from a date.

If this matters for you, the dates are treated as Gregorian dates. Even if they're displayed as some other date type, the year that YEAR will return is the Gregorian-equivalent year for that date.

It's very simple to use. You have a date in a cell and then you use YEAR to reference that cell. So

$$=YEAR(A1)$$

will return the year of the date in Cell A1.

If you reference a date stored as text or written in a text format and formatted as text, Excel will still be able to extract the year for you. Assuming, of course, that the date is a valid date to Excel, so has a year value between 1900 and 9999.

If Excel doesn't recognize the date as a valid date, then it will return a #VALUE! error.

You can also enter the date directly into the function, like so:

$$=YEAR("January 1, 2010")$$

$$=YEAR("1/1/2010")$$

$$=YEAR("1-1-2010")$$

Each of the above will return a value of 2010.

Remember to use the quotation marks or you'll get a #NUM! error message.

Just like the YEAR function extracts the year from a date, the MONTH function extracts the month (as a number between 1 and 12), and the DAY function extracts the day of the month (as a number between 1 and 31).

Also, assuming time of day information is available, the HOUR function extracts the hour (as a number from 0 to 23 because it uses military time), the MINUTE function extracts the minute (as a number from 0 to 59), the SECOND function extracts the second (as a number from 0 to 59).

# The WEEKDAY Function

**Notation:** WEEKDAY(serial_number, [return_type])

**Excel Definition:** Returns a number from 1 to 7 identifying the day of the week of a date.

The WEEKDAY function is another one that's similar to what we just discussed. But this function identifies the day of the week for a specific date. So does it fall on a Monday? A Wednesday? A Sunday? The WEEKDAY function lets you figure that out.

By default the WEEKDAY function returns a number for the day of the week, so a number between 1 and 7, where 1 is equal to Sunday and 7 is equal to Saturday and each day in between is assigned a number value within that range. So

$$=\text{WEEKDAY}(A1)$$

where A1 has January 1, 2019 in it and that date is a Tuesday, will return a value of 3.

You could also write that as

$$=\text{WEEKDAY}("1/1/2019")$$

or

$$=\text{WEEKDAY}("January 1, 2019")$$

If you don't like having Sunday be your first day, you can use the return_type input variable to define a different start point for numbering the days of the week.

Using a return_type value of 2 will assign a value of 1 to Monday instead of Sunday and will then number each day of the week from there ending with a value of 7 for Sunday. So

$$=\text{WEEKDAY}("1/1/2019",2)$$

will return a value of 2 instead of the default value of 3.

Using a value of 3 for return_type assigns a value of 0 to Monday on through to a value of 6 for Sunday. So

$$=\text{WEEKDAY}("January 1, 2019",3)$$

would return a result of 1 since Monday is 0 which makes Tuesday 1.

If you look in the help text for the function you'll see that there's an option for every single day of the week to be your starting point using values from 11 through 17 for return_type.

One way to use this function is to check what day of the week it is and then have different reactions based on that result. So let's say you run an amusement park and you want to have one set of prices, $24.95, for weekday attendees and another price, $29.95, for weekend attendees.

You could write

$$=\text{IF}(\text{WEEKDAY}(A1,11)<6,24.95,29.95)$$

That's saying that using a numbering system where Monday is 1 and Sunday is 7 that if the number of the week is 1 through 5 (or Monday through Friday) then assign a cost of $24.95. If it's not, assign a cost of $29.95.

Done. Works.

# The WEEKNUM Function

**Notation:** WEEKNUM(serial_number, [return_type])

**Excel Definition:** Returns the week number in the year.

The WEEKNUM function is much like the WEEKDAY function except it returns what week of the year a date falls in. So

$$=\text{WEEKNUM}(\text{"January 1, 2019"})$$

will return a value of 1 because that day is in the first week of the year, no matter how you slice or dice it. But, interestingly,

$$=\text{WEEKNUM}(\text{"December 31, 2019"})$$

returns a value of 53 even though there are only 52 weeks in a year.

This is driven by how Excel defines a week.

The default is for Excel to define a week as starting on a Sunday and only including dates for that year. So in 2019 the first week of that year is considered to be January 1st, a Tuesday, through to January 5th, a Saturday. Week 2 of 2019, if you're using the default return type, starts on January 6th, a Sunday. That means that the final days of the year, December 29th through December 31st, fall in the 53rd week of the year.

Under the default, dates in December will always be assigned to their year even if that means that the WEEKNUM result you get back is 53. However, you can use the return_type input option to change how Excel defines a week.

The values of 11 through 17 can be used to start a week on any day from Monday (11) through Sunday (17) but they still keep dates within their year meaning you can still have a week number 53.

There is, however, an option, return_type 21, which follows the ISO 8601 standard for week numbering which is used in Europe. The ISO approach keeps weeks together even if they cross years. It will take the first week of the new year that has a Thursday in it and will then start the week from the Monday of that same week, even if the Monday falls in the prior year. So

$$=WEEKNUM("12/31/2018",21)$$

will return a value of 1, since under the ISO methodology the first week of the year is from December 31, 2018 through January 2, 2019.

Using the return_value of 21 you will never have a week 53 in your results. But you will have end-of-December dates that are assigned to the first week of the next year.

So choose wisely if you use this one.

Also, if you don't want to be bothered to include a return_value of 21 for the WEEKNUM function in order to use the ISO standard, you can just use the ISOWEEKNUM function instead.

# The EDATE Function

**Notation:** EDATE(start_date, months)

**Excel Definition:** Returns the serial number of the date that is the indicated number of months before or after the start date.

The EDATE function takes any given date and gives the date x number of months from that date. So, for example, where the date in Cell B1 is June 15, 2018 and I'm telling Excel to add six months I could just use

$$=\text{EDATE}(B1,6)$$

which gives me a date of December 15, 2018, six months later.

Now, one thing to keep in mind with EDATE is that it will initially return the serial number for the date, so you need to format that cell as a date or your result will be a number. 43449 in this example.

EDATE also works with negative numbers for the number of months. So =EDATE(B1,-6) will give the date six months before the date in Cell B1; in this example that's December 15, 2017.

Note that EDATE returns the exact same date of the month each time, regardless of how many days are in each of the months in between. If for some reason your date is February 29th and you move in a twelve-month increment it will return the 28th.

Also, any month value you use that's not an integer will be truncated not rounded. (So 5.89 would be treated as 5 not 6.)

The EOMONTH function is similar to the EDATE function except it provides the last day of the month x months from your specified date, so December 31, 2018 in our first example above.

# The NETWORKDAYS.INTL Function

**Notation:** NETWORKDAYS.INTL(start_date, end_date, [weekend], [holidays])

**Excel Definition:** Returns the number of whole workdays between two dates with custom weekend parameters.

The NETWORKDAYS.INTL function is a more sophisticated version of NETWORKDAYS and was introduced with Excel 2010. It allows you to take a starting date and an ending date and calculate the number of whole workdays between them, excluding any dates that you classify as holidays.

It's an improvement on NETWORKDAYS because it allows you to specify what constitutes a weekend.

Let's walk through an example. It's December 15, 2020 and I want to know how many workdays there are between now and the end of the year, let's say January 4, 2021.

Let's first just look at the calculation without holidays excluded:

=NETWORKDAYS.INTL("December 15, 2020","January 4, 2021")

The result it gives me is 15.

If I look at my calendar I can see that it's including the 15th as well as January 4th because otherwise there would be three workdays the first week (the 16th, 17th, and 18th) and then five workdays in each of the next two weeks. Only by counting December 15th and January 4th can we get the result of 15.

Not exactly *between* those two dates. It's *inclusive* of the dates you include in your function. Good to know, right?

Now I want to add holidays, but because of the way that NETWORKDAYS.INTL is built, I have to deal with the weekend issue first. For now I'm just going to use a Saturday/Sunday weekend which requires a value of 1. We'll come back to this in a minute.

I don't want to include Christmas or New Year's in the calculation. The easiest way to do this is to have a separate data table where all the holidays to exclude are listed and then use a cell reference.

In this case, I put the dates in Cells C1 and C2, which then gives me:

=NETWORKDAYS.INTL("December 15, 2020","January 4, 2021",1,C1:C2)

where the 1 is my weekend designator and the C1:C2 is my cell range that includes my holidays.

The result I get now is 13 because December 25, 2020 falls on a Friday as does January 1, 2021.

If I don't want the first and last days included, I can combine the function with some basic math and just subtract 2 from my calculated number of days:

=NETWORKDAYS.INTL("December 15, 2020","January 4, 2021",1,C1:C2)-2

In the examples above I used a cell range for my holidays, but how do you include more than one date within the function itself? You have to use curly brackets around your holiday date entries. Like so:

=NETWORKDAYS.INTL("December 15, 2020","January 4, 2021",1,{"12/25/20","1/1/21"})-2

Also note that for every date I listed in the formula above that I had to put quotes around it for Excel to recognize it as a valid date.

Now let's circle back to that third input, the weekend value.

When you get to this point in inputting your values, you will see a dropdown menu of options you can use to specify what days Excel should consider weekends.

Using numbers 11 through 17 allow a single-day weekend and numbers 1 through 7 allow two-day weekends of any consecutive two days in a week.

So let's say that I get off Thursdays and Fridays each week. It looks like this:

=NETWORKDAYS.INTL("December 15, 2020","January 4, 2021",6)

because 6 is the value to use for a Thursday/Friday weekend.
(Interestingly, the result is still 15, but it's using different dates to get there.)
If I expand the function to include my two holidays (which both happen to fall on a Friday), I get this:

=NETWORKDAYS.INTL("December 15, 2020","January 4, 2021",6,{"12/25/20","1/1/21"})

and my result is *still 15*.

Remember with a standard weekend it was 13 because the holidays fell on a workday, but because the holidays in this scenario fall on our "weekend" they've already been excluded from our count of workdays and don't need to be excluded again.

So there you have it. That is how NETWORKDAYS.INTL works.

It also has a counterpart WORKDAY.INTL that calculates what the date will be (January 4, 2021, for example) a specified number of workdays in the future or the past.

Just be advised that unlike NETWORKDAYS.INTL that WORKDAY.INTL does *not* include the present or the final day in its calculation so they are not directly interchangeable.

# Other Functions

That's it for this guide to functions. There are many, many more functions in Excel. Chances are there's at least one I didn't cover here that you will eventually need. But hopefully you now have a good understanding of how the functions work and can use Excel's help to find and structure any function you do need.

I hope this has also given you a taste of the potential power and breadth of Excel. It's a tremendous program that can do so, so much. (You don't have to master all of it, though, to get value from it, so don't feel like you have to keep digging and digging if what you already know now meets your needs.)

Next I want to discuss the various error messages and what they mean and what to do when your formula isn't working.

# When Things Go Wrong

As you start to work with formulas, chances are you're going to run into some errors. I certainly do and I've been at this a long time.

You might see a #/DIV0! or a #REF! or a #VALUE! or a #N/A or a #NUM! error. It happens. Sometimes you'll realize exactly what you did, but at other times it's going to be a puzzle.

So let's me see if I can help a bit.

## #REF!

If you see #REF! in a cell it's probably because you just deleted a value that that cell was referencing. So if you had =A1+B1+C1+D1 in a cell and then you deleted Column C that would create a #REF! error. Excel won't adjust the formula and drop the missing value, it will return this error message instead.

To see where the cell generating the error was in your formula, double-click in the cell with the #REF! message. This will show you the formula, including a #REF! where the missing cell used to be.

So you'll see something like =A1+B1+#REF!+D1 and you'll know that the cell you deleted was used as the third entry in that formula.

If it's something like the example I just gave you where you just need to delete that cell reference, do so. Turn it into =A1+B1+D1. But you may also realize that your formula now needs to reference a different cell. If so, replace the #REF! with that cell reference. Hit enter when you've made your changes and you're done.

## #VALUE!

According to Excel, a #VALUE! error means you typed your formula wrong or you're referencing a cell that's the wrong type of cell.

If you're using dates, see if the date is left-aligned. If it is, then chances are Excel is treating the date as a text entry not a date entry. That means subtraction won't work on it.

Same with numbers. If you use SUM and get this error on a range of numbers make sure that they're formatted as numbers and not text. (This shouldn't be a common problem, but could be if you've imported a data file from elsewhere.)

It can also mean that you have non-standard regional settings and that your minus sign is being used as a list separator (rather than the more standard, at least in the U.S., comma).

Or it can mean that you're referencing a data source that is no longer available like another workbook that was moved.

## #DIV/0!

This is a common error to see if you've written a formula that requires division. If I input the formula =A1/B1 and there are no values in Cells A1 and B1, Excel will return #DIV/0!

You need a numeric value for your denominator to stop this from happening. (The numerator can be blank, but not the denominator.)

I usually use IF functions to suppress the #DIV/0! when I have a data table where values haven't been input yet. So I'll write something like =IF(B1>0,A1/B1,"").

Just be sure if you do that that the IF condition makes sense for your data. (In the example I just gave, any negative number would also result in a blank cell.)

## #N/A

According to Excel, an #N/A error means that Excel isn't finding what it was asked to look for. In other words, there's no solution. This occurs most often with the VLOOKUP, HLOOKUP, and MATCH functions. You tell it to look for a value in your table and that value isn't in your table.

This can be valuable information that perhaps points to a weakness in your data or your function. For example, it could indicate that the data in your lookup table is in a different format from the data in your analysis table. Or that there are extra spaces in the entries in one or the other table

# When Things Go Wrong

But if you know this is going to happen and don't want to see the #N/A in your results, you can use the IFNA function to suppress that result and replace it with a zero, a blank space, or even text.

## #NUM!

According to Excel, you will see this error when there are numeric values in a formula or function that aren't valid. The example Excel gives involves using $1,000 in a formula instead of 1000, but when I just tried this to validate it Excel wouldn't even allow me to use that formula, it wanted to fix the formula for me as soon as I hit Enter. So this may be more of an issue in older versions of Excel.

Excel will also return this error message if an iterative function can't find a result or if the result that would be returned by the formula is too large or too small. (If you're running into this error for those reasons chances are you're doing some pretty advanced things, so we're not going to worry about that here.)

## Circular References

Excel will also flag for you any time that you write a formula that references itself. (I do this on occasion without meaning to.)

For example, if in Cell A5 you type =SUM(A1:A5), Excel will display a dialogue box when you hit Enter that says "Careful, we found one or more circular references in your workbook that might cause your formulas to calculate incorrectly."

Say OK and then go back to the cell with the formula and fix the issue.

Keep in mind that sometimes a circular reference error can be generated by an indirect circular reference, so you're referencing a cell that's referencing another cell and it's that other cell that's the issue.

If you can't figure out the cause and Excel doesn't "helpfully" start drawing connections on your worksheet to show it to you, in newer versions of Excel you can go to the Formulas tab and under Formula Auditing click on Trace Precedents to see what values are feeding that cell.

(Usually when this happens I know exactly what I did and it's just a matter of getting Excel to stop trying to fix it for me so I can make the correction myself.)

## Too Few Arguments

I also on occasion will try to use a function and get a warning message that I've used too few arguments for the function. When that happens check that you've included enough inputs for the function to work. Anything listed that isn't in brackets is required. So =RANDBETWEEN(bottom, top) requires that you enter values for both bottom and top but =CONCATENATE(text1, [text2],…) only requires one input.

If that's not the issue, make sure that you have each of the inputs separated by commas and that your quotation marks and parens are in the right places.

## General Wonkiness

Sometimes everything seems fine but the formula just doesn't seem to be giving the right answer. If it's a complex formula, break it down into its components and make sure that each component works on a standalone basis.

You can also double-click on the cell for a formula and Excel will color code each of the separate components that are feeding the formula and also highlight those cells in your worksheet. Confirm that the highlighted cells are the ones you want.

For formulas you copied, verify that none of your cell ranges or cell references needed to be locked down but weren't. (I do this one often.) If you don't use $ to lock your cell references, they will adjust according to where you copied that formula. If that's what you wanted, great. If it isn't, fix it by going back to the first cell and using the $ signs to lock the cell references and copying and pasting again or by changing the cell references in the location you copied the formula to so that it works.

And, as we've seen here, sometimes there are choices you can make with a function that impact the outcome, like whether you remembered to sort the input range.

If you're working with a function you're not familiar with, open the Excel Help for the function and read through it. That will often give a list of common issues encountered with the function.

# Conclusion

That's it for this guide. There are many more functions that I did not cover here. Excel is incredibly broad in what it can do, but also incredibly specialized at times.

If you can think of it, chances are there's a way to do it in Excel. So don't be afraid to go to Insert Function and poke around to see what's possible.

(And if there isn't a function for what you want, you can always learn how to write your own macros in Excel. Although be careful with those. And don't look to me for that one.)

If you have a specific issue or question, feel free to reach out to me. mlhumphreywriter@gmail.com. I'm happy to help.

Good luck with it! Remember, save your raw data in one place, work on it in another, take your time, check the individual components of complex formulas, check your threshold cases, and Ctrl + Z (Undo) is your friend.

# Appendix A: Cell Notation

If you're going to work with functions in Excel, then you need to understand how Excel references cells.

Cells are referenced based upon their column and their row. So Cell A1 is the cell in Column A and Row 1. Cell B10 is the cell in Column B and Row 10. Cell BC25232 is the cell in Column BC and in Row 25232.

If you want to reference more than one cell or cell range in a function then you can do so in a couple of ways. To reference separate and discrete cells, you list each one and you separate them with a comma. So (A1, A2, A3) refers to Cells A1, A2, and A3.

When cells are touching you can instead reference them as a single range using the colon. So (A1:A3) also refers to Cells A1, A2, and A3. Think of the colon as a "through".

You don't have to limit this to a single row or column either. You can reference A1:B25. That refers to all of the cells between Cell A1 and Cell B25. That would be all cells in Column A from Cell A1 through Cell A25 as well as all cells in Column B from Cell B1 through Cell B25.

When you note a range best practice is for the left-hand cell that you list (A1) to be the top left-most cell of the range and the right-hand cell you list (B25) to be the bottom right-most cell of the range.

You can also reference an entire column by using the letter and leaving off any numbers. So C:C refers to all cells in Column C.

And you can do the same for a row by leaving off the letter. So 10:10 refers to all the cells in Row 10.

If you ever reference a cell in another worksheet or another workbook, this also needs to be addressed through cell notation.

For a cell in another worksheet, you put the sheet name as it appears on the worksheet tab followed by an exclamation point before the cell reference. So Sheet1!B1 is Cell B1 in the worksheet labeled Sheet 1.

For another workbook you put the name of the workbook in brackets before the worksheet name. So [Book1]Sheet2!$D$2 refers to Cell D2 in the worksheet labeled Sheet 2 in the workbook titled Book 1.

(I should note here that I think it's a bad idea to reference data in another workbook due to the odds that the formula/function will break as soon as that other workbook is renamed or moved to a new location and that I generally don't think it's worth doing.)

Now, before you start to panic and think you need to remember all of this and that you never will, take a deep breath. Because when you're writing a formula you can simply click on the cells you need when you need them and Excel will write the cell notation for you.

It's just useful to know how this works in case something doesn't work right. (And even then you can still use Excel to show you what each cell reference is referring to. Just double-click on the formula and Excel will color code the cell references in the formula and put a matching colored border around the cells in your worksheet.)

# Index of Functions

**A**
- ABS 140
- AND 51–52
- AVERAGE 58–59, 124
- AVERAGEA 60–61
- AVERAGEIFS 87–89

**C**
- CHOOSE 106–107
- COMBIN 147
- COMBINA 147
- CONCAT 37
- CONCATENATE 37
- CONVERT 34–36
- COUNT 62, 129
- COUNTA 63
- COUNTBLANK 63
- COUNTIF 82
- COUNTIFS 80–83

**D**
- DATE 163–166
- DAY 165, 168

**E**
- EDATE 173
- EOMONTH 173
- EXACT 158
- EXP 142, 144

**F**
- FACT 146
- FALSE 70
- FORECAST.ETS 132
- FORECAST.LINEAR 130–132
- FREQUENCY 133–135

**H**
- HLOOKUP 100–102
- HOUR 168

**I**
- IF 71, 73, 77–79, 97, 170
- IFERROR 97, 98
- IFNA 94–96
- IFS 45–49
- INDEX 110–116
- ISOWEEKNUM 172

**L**
- LARGE 129
- LEFT 104, 151, 157
- LEFTB 152
- LEN 156–157
- LN 145
- LOG 144
- LOG10 145
- LOWER 150

**M**
- MATCH 116–117
- MAX 66
- MAXA 66
- MAXIFS 92–93
- MEDIAN 120–122, 124
- MID 153
- MIDB 152
- MIN 64
- MINA 65
- MINIFS 90–91
- MINUTE 168
- MODE.MULT 123–125, 133
- MODE.SNGL 122, 124
- MONTH 165, 168

**N**
- NA 71
- NETWORKDAYS 174
- NETWORKDAYS.INTL 174–176
- NOT 72–73
- NOW 44

**O**
- OR 68, 69

**P**
- PI 143
- POWER 141–142
- PRODUCT 138
- PROPER 150

**R**
- RAND 32
- RANDBETWEEN 32–33
- RANK 126
- RANK.AVG 127
- RANK.EQ 126–127
- RIGHT 152
- RIGHTB 152
- ROUND 29–31
- ROUNDDOWN 31
- ROUNDUP 31

**S**
- SECOND 168
- SMALL 128–129
- SQRT 142
- SQRTPI 142
- SUM 26–28
- SUMIF 84
- SUMIFS 84–86
- SUMPRODUCT 1, 138–139
- SWITCH 103–105

**T**
- TEXT 103, 154–155
- TEXTJOIN 37–40, 150
- TODAY 43, 44
- TRANSPOSE 108–109, 115
- TRIM 40–42
- TRUE 70
- TRUNC 31

**U**
- UPPER 150

**V**
- VLOOKUP 53–55, 95, 102

**W**
- WEEKDAY 103, 107, 169–170
- WEEKNUM 171–172
- WORKDAY.INTL 176

**X**
- XLOOKUP 102

**Y**
- YEAR 165–168

# About the Author

M.L. Humphrey is a former stockbroker with a degree in Economics from Stanford and an MBA from Wharton who has spent close to twenty years as a regulator and consultant in the financial services industry.

You can reach M.L. Humphrey at:

mlhumphreywriter@gmail.com

or at

www.mlhumphrey.com

Printed in Great Britain
by Amazon